Now That You've Had a Home Inspection...

Now that you've bought your home and had your inspection, you may still have some questions about your new house and the items revealed in your report.

Home maintenance is a primary responsibility for every homeowner, whether you've lived in several homes of your own or have just purchased your first one. Staying on top of a seasonal home maintenance schedule is important, and your InterNACHI Certified Professional Inspector® can help you figure this out so that you never fall behind. Don't let minor maintenance and routine repairs turn into expensive disasters later due to neglect or simply because you aren't sure what needs to be done and when.

Your home inspection report is a great place to start. In addition to the written report, checklists, photos, and what the inspector himself said during the inspection—not to mention the seller's disclosure and what you noticed yourself—it's easy to become overwhelmed. However, it's likely that your inspection report included mostly maintenance recommendations, the life expectancy for the home's various systems and components, and minor imperfections. These are useful to know about.

The issues that really matter fall into four categories:

1. major defects, such as a structural failure;
2. things that can lead to major defects, such as a small leak due to a defective roof flashing;
3. things that may hinder your ability to finance, legally occupy, or insure the home if not rectified immediately; and
4. safety hazards, such as an exposed, live buss bar at the electrical panel.

Anything in these categories should be addressed as soon as possible. Often, a serious problem can be corrected inexpensively to protect both life and property (especially in categories 2 and 4).

Most sellers are honest and are often surprised to learn of defects uncovered during an inspection. It's important to realize that sellers are under no obligation to repair everything mentioned in your inspection report. No house is perfect. Keep things in perspective as you move into your new home.

And remember that homeownership is both a joyful experience and an important responsibility, so be sure to call on your InterNACHI Certified Professional Inspector® to help you devise an annual maintenance plan that will keep your family safe and your home in top condition for years to come.

My Inspector:

The purpose of this publication is to provide accurate and useful information in regard to the maintenance of a residential building. Before acting on the information contained in this book, consult a qualified contractor.

Neither the publisher nor author is engaged in rendering legal, accounting, construction, repair or other professional service. If legal advice or other expert assistance is needed, the services of a professional should be sought.

Neither the publisher nor author is liable or responsible in any way for the specific use of any of the information in this book.

WARNING: Maintenance involves risk of bodily injury and to personal property. Do not perform repairs or corrections by yourself. Before performing any maintenance or work on your house, hire an appropriately qualified contractor. Do not act upon the information provided in this book without consulting an expert or qualified contractor.

This book does not come with a warranty of any kind.

To order:
Visit us at www.nachi.org/go/nowbook

Written by:
Benjamin Gromicko

Edited by:
Kate Tarasenko / Crimea River, LLC

Graphics by:
Lisaira Vega, Levi Nelson & Erica Saurey

Layout & Design by:
Jessica Langer

www.NACHI.org

 InterNACHI®, the International Association of Certified Home Inspectors, is the world's largest nonprofit association of residential property inspectors. InterNACHI® provides its members with education, training, and support. An InterNACHI® Certified Professional Inspector® is the most qualified home inspector you can hire!

InterNACHI® inspectors:

- abide by a strict Code of Ethics, which puts your interests first;

- follow a comprehensive Standards of Practice, which ensures that you receive a comprehensive and accurate home inspection;

- are required to stay up to date with the industry's most rigorous Continuing Education and training courses, which have been approved and accredited by hundreds of state and governmental agencies, including the U.S. Department of Education; and

- use state-of-the-art tools and reporting software, all to provide you with the best inspection experience to help you make an informed decision about the home you want to buy or sell.

Don't forget to have your InterNACHI® inspector back next year for your Annual Home Maintenance Inspection!

Table of Contents

Nice house! As your home inspector, I'm here to guide you through the important tasks that come with owning a home. Follow me through this book as I give you helpful tips for monitoring your house and recognizing the warning signs that will alert you to potential problems. Contact your InterNACHI-Certified Professional Inspector® if you have any questions. And don't forget to sign up for your home maintenance newsletter for more helpful tips!

Just like the engine of an automobile, your house works as a system of interdependent parts. Every part has an impact on the operation of many other parts. A typical home has over 10,000 parts. What happens when all the parts work together in the most desirable, optimal way? You are rewarded with a house that is durable, comfortable, healthy and energy-efficient.

You can make it happen in just a few steps:

Step #1: Monitor the house.

Step #2: Recognize potential problems.

Step #3: Correct problems properly.

This book will help you do all three steps.

If you hired an InterNACHI-Certified Professional Inspector®, that was a good decision and money well spent.

As you know, the home inspector is not an expert but a generalist. Your home inspector inspected the home and reported the home's condition as it was at the time of the inspection. That is the main responsibility of the home inspector. A home inspection does not include predictions of future events. Future events (such as roof leaks, water intrusion, plumbing drips and heating failures) are not within the scope of a home inspection and are not the responsibility of the home inspector.

Who's responsible? You are, the new homeowner. Welcome to homeownership. The most important thing to understand as a new homeowner is that things break. As time goes on, parts of your house will wear out, break down, deteriorate, leak, or simply stop working.

But relax. Don't get overwhelmed. You're not alone. This book is for you and every homeowner experiencing the responsibility of homeownership. Every homeowner has similar concerns and questions. And they are all related to home maintenance.

The following questions are those that all homeowners ask themselves:

#1 "What should I look for?"

#2 "What does a real problem look like?"

#3 "How should it be corrected?"

The answers to these questions are written in this book. This book will guide you through the systems of a typical house, how they work and how to maintain them. The systems include the following: the exterior, interior, roof, structure, electrical, HVAC, plumbing, attic and insulation.

You will learn what to monitor as the house ages. Most of the conditions and events that you will see and experience will likely be cosmetic and minor in nature. Most homes do not have major material defects.

Throughout the book, there are references to the International Association of Certified Home Inspectors (www.nachi.org). InterNACHI is the world's largest association of residential and commercial property inspectors. The InterNACHI Residential Standards of Practice (SOP) defines what a home inspection is and lists the responsibilities of a home inspector. The SOP can be viewed at www.nachi.org/go/sop. Be sure to read the Standards of Practice to which your inspection is performed.

This book comments upon the responsibilities of a home inspector because we are assuming that a home inspector has given you this book to read. Sometimes, when a new homeowner is performing maintenance, apparent problems are discovered or revealed. Or, as time goes by, things in the house leak or fail. A new homeowner experiencing a problem should refer to the Standards of Practice, which outlines the responsibilities and limitations of the home inspector.

Some of the topics of this book include:

- the systems and components of a typical house;

- how to save energy;

- how to make your home more comfortable and energy-efficient by sealing air leaks and adding insulation—and you can do it yourself;

- maintenance checklists for each season; and

- the average life expectancies of systems, components and appliances in a typical home.

Homeownership is a great experience, and home maintenance is a great responsibility. This book will help you enjoy both.

Enjoy your house!

Chapter 1: InterNACHI Standards of Practice

The Residential Standards of Practice of the International Association of Certified Home Inspectors can be read in its entirety at **www.nachi.org/go/sop**. Throughout this book, the Standards are referenced and abbreviated. The complete version is not printed in this book.

According to the Standards of Practice, a home inspection is a non-invasive, visual examination of a residential dwelling, performed for a fee, which is designed to identify observed material defects within specific components of said dwelling. Components may include any combination of mechanical, structural, electrical, plumbing and/or other essential systems or portions of the home, as identified and agreed to by the client and inspector prior to the inspection process.

There's no crystal ball. A home inspection is intended to assist in evaluation of the overall condition of the dwelling. The inspection is based on observations of the visible and apparent condition of the structure and its components on the date of the inspection, and not the prediction of future conditions.

You may later find problems in your house that were not identified in your home inspection report. That's because a home inspection will not reveal every problem that exists or ever could exist, but only those material defects that were observed on the day of the inspection.

A "material defect" is a specific issue with a system or component of a residential property that may have a significant, adverse impact on the value of the property, or that poses an unreasonable risk to people. The fact that a system or component is near, at or beyond the end of its normal useful life is not, in itself, a material defect.

An inspection report describes and identifies, in written format, the inspected systems, structures and components of the dwelling, and identifies the material defects that the inspector observed. Your inspection report may contain recommendations regarding the conditions reported and/or suggestions for correction, monitoring or further evaluation by professionals, but this is not required by the inspector, according to the Standards of Practice.

Chapter 2: Site and Environment

2.1 Property Drainage

During a heavy rainstorm (without lightning), grab an umbrella and go outside. Walk around your house and look around at the roof and property. A rainstorm is the perfect time to see how the roof, downspouts and grading are performing. Observe the drainage patterns of your entire property, as well as the property of your neighbor. The ground around your house should slope away from all sides. Downspouts, surface gutters and drains should be directing water away from the foundation.

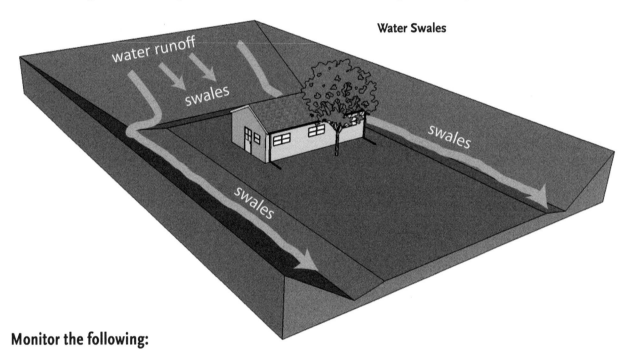

Monitor the following:

Poor drainage. Most problems with moisture in basements and crawlspaces are caused by poor site drainage. The ground should slope away from window wells, outside basement stairs, and other means of egress. The bottom of each of these areas should be sloped to a drain. Each drain should have piping that connects it to a stormwater drainage system (if there is one) or that drains to either a discharge at a lower grade or into a sump pit that collects and discharges the water away from the building.

 Your job is to monitor and maintain the drains and piping. Drains and piping should be open and clear of leaves, earth and debris. A garden hose can be used to check water flow,

although its discharge cannot approximate storm conditions.

Hillside. Where a building is situated on a hillside, it is more difficult to slope the ground away from the building on all sides. On the high-ground side of the building, the slope of the ground toward the building could be interrupted by a surface drainage system that collects and disposes of rainwater runoff. Swales can be used to direct surface water away from the foundation. There are two general types of surface drainage systems: an open system, consisting of a swale (often referred to as a ditch), sometimes with a culvert at its end to collect and channel water away; and a closed system, consisting of gutters with catch basins.

Planters. Check any planting beds adjacent to the foundation. They are built in a way that traps water. The structure around the planting beds acts like a dam and traps water. Flower planters should never be installed up against a house's exterior wall.

Puddles are not good. The ground surface beneath decks, porches and other parts of a building that are supported by posts or cantilevered structures should be checked. It should not have any low-lying areas, but should be sloped so that water will not collect and puddle there. Settled backfill allows water to collect next to the foundation wall and penetrate into the basement.

Downspouts need adjustment. Water from the roof reaches the ground through gutters and downspouts or by flowing directly off roof edges. Because downspouts create concentrated sources of water in the landscape, where they discharge is important. Downspouts should not discharge where water will flow directly on or over a walkway, driveway or stairs. The downspouts on a hillside building should discharge on the downhill side of the building. The force of water leaving a downspout is sometimes great enough to damage the adjacent ground, so some protection at grade, such as a splash block or a paved drainage chute, is needed. In urban areas, it is better to drain downspouts to an underground stormwater drainage system, if there is one, or underground to discharge at a lower grade away from buildings.

Water that flows directly off a roof lacking gutters and downspouts can cause damage below. Accordingly, some provision in the landscaping may be needed, such as a gravel bed or paved drainage way.

The sump pump should not recycle. When a sump pump is used to keep a building's interior dry, the discharge should drain away from the building and should not add to the subsurface water condition that the sump pump is meant to control.

Naturally wet. Look around the entire site for the presence of springs, standing water, saturated or boggy ground, a high water table, or dry creeks or other seasonal drainage ways, all of which may affect surface drainage.

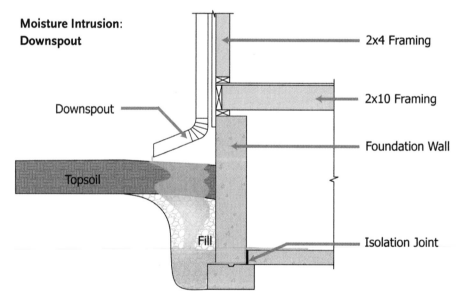

Moisture Intrusion:
Downspout

Downspout

Topsoil

Fill

2x4 Framing

2x10 Framing

Foundation Wall

Isolation Joint

2.2 Landscaping

Well-maintained landscaping and other improvements are important for the enjoyment of a healthy and durable property.

Monitor the following:

Plants, Trees & Shrubs. Check the location and condition of all trees and shrubbery. Those that are overgrown should be pruned or trimmed. Where trees or bushes have overgrown, complete removal may be necessary.

Trees need to be trimmed. Overhanging branches should not interfere with a chimney's draft, damage utility wires, or deposit leaves and twigs on the roof, or inside gutters and drains. Trees and shrubbery that are very close to exterior walls or roofs can cause damage. They can make it difficult to perform homeowner maintenance inspections and repairs. Branches around the perimeter of the house should be pruned back. Tree roots under concrete walks can cause damage. Roots are usually exposed near the surface and can be cut back. Tree roots can cause foundations to crack by pushing against foundations from the outside. Consider hiring an arborist. An arborist is a specialist in the cultivation and care of trees and shrubs, including tree surgery, the diagnosis, treatment, and prevention of tree diseases, and the control of pests. Find a certified arborist in the U.S. at **www.nachi.org/go/arborists** and **www.nachi.org/go/caforests** in Canada.

Foundation Failure: Tree Root

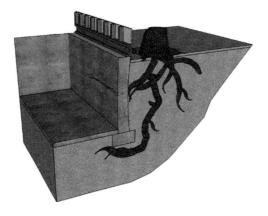

Fences fall apart and lean over. Fences are usually installed to provide physical or visual privacy. Fences should be plumb and in good repair.

Check wooden fences for development of rot or insect infestation. Check metal fences for rust development. All gates and their hardware should have proper fittings, operation and clearances. Fences are often addressed in homeowner association bylaws and deed covenants. Pay special attention to fence locations and your property lines. Neighbors can get quite un-neighborly about property lines.

Concrete pavement cracks and settlement. Monitor paved areas. Where there is a difference in elevation in a walk or driveway that creates a tripping hazard, the higher portion of concrete may be ground down to the level of the lower portion, although the grinding will change the appearance of the concrete. Paved areas immediately adjacent to a building should slope away from the perimeter of the building walls (foundation walls). Paving that is not sloped to drain water away from a building should be repaired. Repair any paving that has large cracks, broken sections, high areas, low areas that trap water, and tripping hazards. Repairing concrete often requires total replacement. Resurfacing with a thin layer of more concrete cannot repair concrete. Concrete should be no less than 3 inches thick. Cracks in concrete can be cut open and sealed with a flexible-sealant compound, which will extend its service life. For sidewalks that have settled downward, it may be possible to lift up sections.

Asphalt surface. Sealing asphalt paving extends its life. Homeowners should seal-coat their asphalt driveways every three to five years. Examine the paving to determine when sealing is needed. Check asphalt driveways for sunken areas that hold water. Low areas in asphalt paving can be brought to level with an asphalt repair.

Paving. Paving does not last forever. Brick or stone patio paving could be set on a concrete slab, in a mortar bed with mortar joints, or in a sand bed that is laid on earth. Mortar joints can be tuck-pointed. Loose bricks or stones can be reset in a new mortar bed. Pavers set in sand can be taken up easily, sand added or removed, and the pavers replaced. The maintenance and repair of sidewalks, driveway aprons and curbs at the street may be your responsibility or that of the local jurisdiction.

Exterior steps. Check the condition of exterior stairs and railings. Every once in a while, shake all railings vigorously to check their stability and inspect their fastenings. Every stair with more than three steps should have a handrail located 34 to 38 inches above the edges of the stair tread.

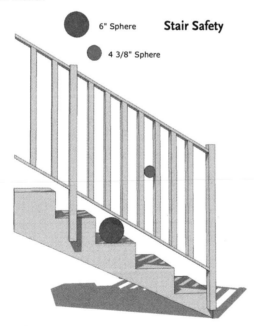

6" Sphere
4 3/8" Sphere
Stair Safety

Stairs that are more than 30 inches above the adjacent grade and walks located more than 30 inches above the grade immediately below should have guards not less than 36 inches high and intermediate rails that do not allow

the passage of a sphere 4 inches in diameter. Wooden steps should have proper support and strength, and no rot or insect infestation should be allowed to develop. At steel stairs, look for the development of rust, weakened strength or poor attachment. Deteriorated stairs should be repaired or replaced. Stair treads should be as level as possible without holding water. Stair riser heights and tread depths should be uniform.

Retaining walls. If possible, weep holes and related drains should be looked at following a heavy rain to make sure they are working properly. If they are not discharging water, the drains should be cleaned out and observed again in the next rain. Retaining walls more than 2 feet in height should be backed with drainage material, such as gravel. There should be drains at the bottom of the drainage material. The drains should discharge water either at the end of the wall or through pipes. These drains and the drainage material behind the wall relieve the pressure of groundwater on the wall. Failure to drain could be remedied by excavating behind the wall, replacing the drainage material and damaged drainage piping, and backfilling. In all but the driest climates, improper drainage of water from behind a retaining wall can cause the wall to fail.

Look for movement in your retaining walls. Bowing (vertical bulges), sweeping (horizontal bulges), and cracking in retaining walls can be caused by water pressure (or hydrostatic pressure). Bulging can also be a result of inadequate strength to resist the load of the earth behind the wall. Bowing and sweeping failures may be correctable if found early enough and if the cause is poor drainage.

There are other types of failures of retaining walls. Failure by over-turning (leaning from the top) or sliding may be caused by inadequate wall strength. In addition, water behind a wall can create unstable earth, especially in clay soils, and contribute to sliding. Retaining walls also fail due to settlement and heaving. Settlement occurs whenever filled earth below the wall compacts soon after the wall is built, or when wet earth caused by poor drainage dries out and soil consolidates. Poor drainage contributes to failure in cold climates by creating heaving from frozen ground. Both overturning and sliding may be stabilized and sometimes corrected if the amount of movement is not extreme. Settling may be corrected on small, low walls of concrete or masonry, and heaving may be controlled by proper drainage. Significant failure of any kind usually requires rebuilding or replacing all or part of a wall. Consult a qualified professional when major repairs or corrections are needed.

Inspecting Retaining Walls

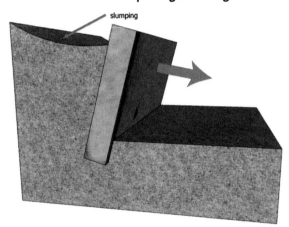

Buried oil tanks. A buried oil tank can be covered up by heavy landscaping. Buried ferrous-metal oil tanks are commonly found on older properties whose home and/or domestic water supply is heated by oil. The presence of a buried oil tank can usually be determined by finding the fill and vent pipes that extend above ground. Abandoned and very old buried ferrous-metal oil tanks are an environmental hazard. If you have a buried tank on the property, the soil around it should be tested by a qualified environmental professional for the presence of oil seepage. If leaking has occurred, the tank and all contaminated soil around it must be removed. If leaking has not occurred, it may still be a potential problem. Even if a tank is empty, it still may have residual oil in the bottom that is a pollutant.

Note: As with all underground items, a buried oil tank is not within the scope of a visual home inspection.

2.3 Other Structures

Keep detached garages, storage sheds and other outbuildings in good condition in the same way that your home is maintained. Monitor each outbuilding's water-shedding capability and the adequacy of its foundation. Look for roof leaks from inside the buildings. Wood frame structures should be checked for rot and insect infestation. Check that doors and windows provide adequate weather protection and security for the buildings. Small outbuildings should have sufficient structural strength to sustain wind loads or seismic forces—this may be more than just a simple judgment call. If the site is in a hurricane or high-wind region, check all outbuildings for their ability to resist a storm without coming apart and becoming windborne debris. Consider consulting a qualified professional.

2.4 Yards and Courts

In urban areas, two or more dwelling units may share a yard or court to provide light and ventilation to interior rooms. The adequacy of the light provided to the interior rooms of the home may be a function of the dimensions of the yard or court. Check these characteristics, as well as zoning and building and housing code requirements pertaining to light, ventilation, and privacy screening for yards and courts. Such requirements may affect the reuse of the property, and their implications should be understood before the property is altered.

2.5 Flood Zones

Check with local authorities to determine if your home is in a flood-risk zone. If it is, check with local building officials. Higher standards than those set by national agencies have been adopted by many communities.

The Federal Emergency Management Agency (FEMA) and the National Flood Insurance Program have established and defined five major flood-risk zones and created special flood-resistance requirements for each. For a flood map, visit **www.nachi.org/go/femamaps**. Improperly designed grading and drainage may aggravate flood hazards to buildings and cause runoff, soil erosion and sedimentation in the zones of lower flood risk, according to the Interflood Zone and the Non-Regulated Flood Plain. In these locations, local agencies may regulate building elevations above street or sewer levels. In the next higher risk zones, the Special Flood Hazard Areas and the Non-Velocity Coastal Flood Areas (both Zone A), the elevation of the lowest floor and its structural members above the base flood elevation is required. In the zone of highest flood risk, the Coastal High Hazard Areas (Velocity Zone, Zone V), additional structural requirements apply.

2.6 Other Factors

The following are several factors about a home and its property that are often overlooked.

Grading. Look at the property around the house and the slope of the ground. If your house is on a ground slope of 20 degrees or more (in all seismic regions, including regions of low seismic activity), a structural engineer should be considered to further examine the building in relation to the slope.

Wind. Look for loose fences, tree limbs, and landscaping materials, such as gravel and small rocks, and other objects that could become windborne debris in a storm, if the building is in a hurricane or high-wind region.

Solid Fence Wind Protection

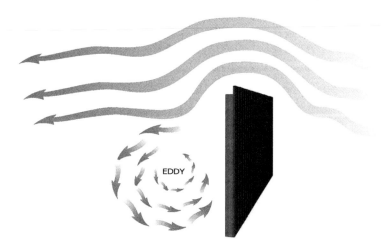

EDDY

Floods. Check with local authorities. Major flood-risk zones have been established to define where floods occur, and special flood-resistance requirements have been created for each zone.

Lead. Consider checking for the presence of lead in the soil, which can be a hazard to children playing outdoors and can be tracked indoors on shoes. Lead in soil can come from different sources, such as discarded lead-based paint, lead-based paint chips at the perimeter of stone foundations where the paint is flaking, and old trash sites where items containing lead were discarded.

Consider having the soil and home tested for lead by a qualified professional inspector. For more information, consult your inspector and visit: **www.nachi.org/go/epalead**

Wildfires. In locations where wildfires can occur, some jurisdictions have requirements for hydrant locations and restrictions on the use of certain building materials, as well as restrictions on plantings close to a building.

In the context of fire control, defensible space is the area around a structure that has been landscaped to reduce fire danger. Check with the local building official and the fire marshal for such requirements.

Construction Expansion. If a future construction project on the house includes expansion, an assessment of the site for this future work is critical. The use of the land around the existing house is likely restricted by coverage and set-back requirements, which define the areas of the property that can be used for future construction projects.

Site Restrictions. Homeowner association bylaws and deed covenants sometimes include requirements that can affect changes or additions to a building or outbuilding.

Accessibility. When universal design is a need, consult a code-certified professional inspector for detailed information about parking, walkways, patios and egress.

According to the Standards of Practice:

The inspector is responsible for checking the roof gutters, downspouts and surface drainage, but is not responsible for inspecting any underground drainage pipes. The inspector is not required to inspect erosion control, earth-stabilization measures, or geological or soil conditions.

Chapter 3: Sloped Roof Coverings

Monitor the roof covering because any roof can leak. To monitor a roof that is inaccessible or that cannot be walked on safely, use binoculars. Look for deteriorating or loosening of flashing, signs of damage to the roof covering and debris that can clog valleys and gutters.

Carefully watch the exterior walls and trim for deterioration developing beneath the eaves of pitched roofs that have no overhang or gutters.

Roofs are designed to be water-resistant. Roofs are not designed to be waterproof. Eventually, the roof system will leak. No one can predict when, where or how a roof will leak.

Hail and wind damage. Hail and wind can cause significant damage to your asphalt shingle roof. After a storm, consider hiring a reputable roofing contractor or certified home inspector to evaluate the condition of your shingle roof. There's no need for you to risk your life doing something that an experienced professional does every day. Hail and wind damage may likely be covered by your homeowner's insurance policy.

Thermography. An infrared camera can be used to detect areas of moisture at roof structures. Once located, these areas can be more thoroughly checked with a moisture-metering device. Such evaluations must be performed by an inspector who is trained in infrared technology and building science. Consult your inspector.

There are four general categories of pitched roof-covering materials, and their condition should be monitored as follows:

Asphalt shingles. Asphalt or composition shingles have a service life from 15 to 40 years, depending on the shingle quality, installation and maintenance. When they begin to lose their granular covering and start to curl, the shingles should be replaced. No more than two layers of asphalt shingles should be in place

at any one time. If a second layer of asphalt shingles has been applied, check to see if all the flashing materials of the first layer were removed and replaced with new flashing at the second layer.

Asphalt Shingles

The roof slope. The slope (sometimes called pitch) of a roof is expressed as a ratio of the rise (vertical distance) over the run (horizontal distance). The run is usually expressed as 12, and a typical slope might be 4 in 12 or 6 in 12. A slope of 4 in 12 or steeper is referred to as normal. A slope of between 3 in 12 and 4 in 12 is referred to as low. A 45-degree roof slope would have a pitch of 12 in 12. Typically, asphalt shingle roofs should not have a slope of less than 4 in 12.

Underlayment. There should be underlayment installed. It should be at least a single layer of 15-pound asphalt-saturated felt. Low-slope roofs should have at least two such felt layers. If ice-dam flashing at overhanging eaves is needed or present, there should be additional measures taken and particular underlayment materials applied. The number of underlayment layers and the installation of underlayment are difficult to observe and would only need to be investigated if water intrusion occurs.

Wood shingles and shakes. This type of covering has a normal life expectancy of 20 to 30 years in climates that are not excessively hot and humid. Durability varies according to wood species, thickness, the slope of the roof, and whether the shingles are made of heartwood. Maintenance may include periodically treating the shingles with preservative.

Shakes are hand-split on at least one face and either tapered or straight. Shingles are sawn and tapered. They should not be walked on. These materials are easily broken. The minimum slope for wood shingles is 3 in 12 and the minimum slope for shakes is 4 in 12. As wood shingles and shakes age, they dry, crack and curl. In damp locations they rot. When more than one-third shows signs of deterioration, consider replacing them.

Metal roofing. Metal can last 50 years or more if properly painted or otherwise maintained. Metal roofs may be made of galvanized iron or steel, aluminum, copper or lead. Each material has its own unique wearing characteristics.

Monitor metal roofs for the development of rusting or pitting, corrosion due to galvanic reaction, and loose, open or leaking seams or joints. The types of metal, seams and slope determine the construction details. There are three basic seam types: batten, standing, and flat. There are also flat and formed metal panels.

The slope of metal roofing can be from ½-inch per foot (1:24) to very steep. Snow guards on roofs with steeper slopes should be installed. In locations with heavy, long-lasting snow, bracket and pipe snow guards also may be necessary.

Low-slope metal roofs that are coated with tar-like material are probably patched or have pinholes and cannot be counted on to be water-resistant.

Shingles: Spaced Sheathing

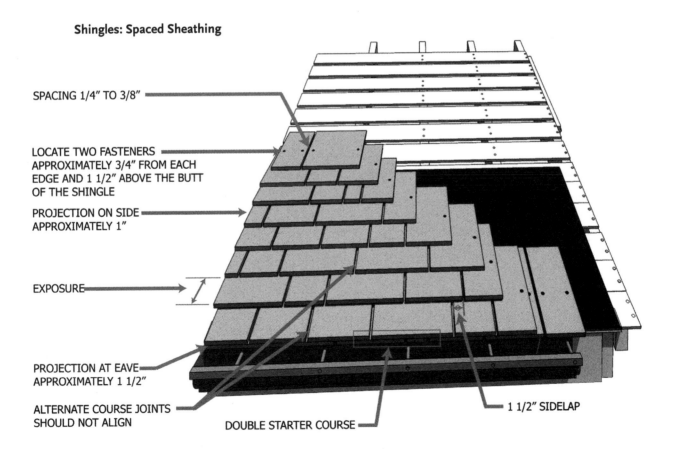

SPACING 1/4" TO 3/8"

LOCATE TWO FASTENERS APPROXIMATELY 3/4" FROM EACH EDGE AND 1 1/2" ABOVE THE BUTT OF THE SHINGLE

PROJECTION ON SIDE APPROXIMATELY 1"

EXPOSURE

PROJECTION AT EAVE APPROXIMATELY 1 1/2"

ALTERNATE COURSE JOINTS SHOULD NOT ALIGN

DOUBLE STARTER COURSE

1 1/2" SIDELAP

Slate, clay tile, and asbestos cement shingles. These roof coverings are extremely durable and, if of high quality and properly maintained, may last the life of the structure. The minimum slope for roofs of these materials is 4 in 12. Slate shingles should be secured by copper nails except in the very driest of climates. Nail heads could be covered with sealant. Nails for tile roofs should be non-corroding.

All of these roof coverings are brittle materials, are easily broken, and should not be walked on. Use binoculars to look for missing, broken or slipping pieces. Slate is particularly susceptible to breakage by ice or ice dams in the winter. You should have snow guards on steeper slopes, and in locations with heavy, long-lasting snow, snow guards may also be necessary. Moss will sometimes grow on asbestos cement shingles, but it can be removed with a cleaner to prevent capillary water leaks. Slate, clay tile, and asbestos shingles should be repaired or replaced by a qualified roofer.

Clay and Slate Shingles

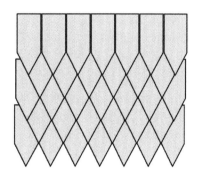 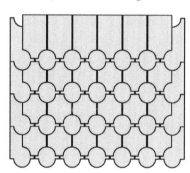 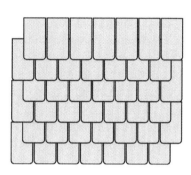

a few of the many different patterns used with clay and slate shingles

3.1 Low-Slope Roof Coverings

A roof that is nearly level or slightly pitched is called a low-slope roof. No roof should be actually level and flat; it must have at least a slight slope to properly drain. Low-slope roofs can be expensive to repair, so care should be taken in their maintenance.

 **Regular maintenance and periodic inspections for low-slope roofs are necessary.** Problems with low-slope roofs are common and more difficult to diagnose than pitched roof problems because the path of water leakage through flat roofs is often quite hard to trace.

Watch for signs of ponding water (or puddle formation) on the surface due to either improper drainage or sagging of the roof deck. If the cause is a sagging deck, it should be structurally corrected.

Monitor the flashing and joints around all roof penetrations, including drains, soil stacks, chimneys, skylights, hatchways, antenna mountings, and other roof-mounted elements.

Check to see if metal flashings need painting or re-anchoring, and if asphalt or rubber flashings are brittle or cracked. Parapet wall caps and flashing may develop damage due to wall movement or moisture.

There are four categories of low-slope roof-covering materials, and they should be monitored as follows:

Built-up roofing (BUR). Built-up roofs are composed of several layers of roofing felt that is lapped, cemented together with bituminous material, and protected by a thin layer of gravel or crushed stone. Built-up roofs vary greatly in life span, but those used in residential buildings usually last about 20 years, depending on their quality, exposure, number of plies, and the adequacy of their drainage.

Because built-up roofs are composed of several layers, they can hold moisture in the form of water or water vapor between layers. Moisture not only accelerates deterioration, it can also leak into a building.

Regular maintenance and periodic inspections are necessary. Look for cracking, blistering, alligatoring and wrinkling, all of which may indicate the need for roof replacement or repair. Consult an experienced roofer or your home inspector for further evaluation if you have doubt about the roof's apparent condition.

Single-ply membrane roofing. A single-ply membrane roof consists of plastic, modified bitumen and synthetic rubber sheeting that is laid over the roof deck, usually in a single ply, and often with a top coating to protect it from ultraviolet light degradation. Single-ply roofs are installed in three basic ways: fully adhered; mechanically attached; and loose-laid with ballast. If properly installed and maintained, a single-ply roof should last 20 years.

Roof penetrations and seams are the most vulnerable parts of single-ply membrane roofing and should be carefully monitored. The material is also susceptible to ultraviolet light deterioration. A protective coating can be applied, but it will need to be reapplied periodically. Check carefully for surface degradation on an unprotected roof and fading of the coating on a protected roof. Check also for signs of water ponding and poor drainage.

Roll roofing. Roll roofing should be inspected before and after the winter season. Roll roofing consists of an asphalt-saturated, granule-covered roofing felt that is laid over the roof deck. Inspect roll roofing for cracking, blistering, surface erosion, and torn sections. Seams are the most vulnerable part of roll roofing and should be carefully checked for separation and lifting. Also, check for signs of water ponding and poor drainage.

3.2 Parapets and Gables

In seismic zones, check the bracing of masonry parapets and gables. Consider consulting a structural engineer to determine the need for additional bracing or strengthening.

3.3 Skylights

A leaking skylight is a common experience. From outside, watch the glazing for cracks or breaks, loosening of the flashing, and rusting or decaying frames. Skylights should be checked from the interior, too. Don't be surprised if your skylight develops a leak.

3.4 Gutters and Downspouts

All gutters need to be kept clean. They should slope uniformly, without sags, to downspouts. Gutter and downspout materials are usually galvanized steel, aluminum, copper or plastic.

Buildings with pitched roofs can have a variety of drainage systems. With a sufficient overhang, water can drain directly to the ground without being collected at the roof edge.

Drainage of low-slope roofs is accomplished in one of three ways: without gutters or downspouts; with gutters and downspouts; or by downspouts that go down through a building's interior. Drainage without gutters and downspouts can damage the exterior wall with overflow. If the roof has no gutters and downspouts or interior downspouts, carefully monitor the exterior walls for signs of water damage.

Most functional gutters have a minimum ratio of gutter depth to width of 3 to 4. The front edge is typically ½-inch lower than the back edge. Four inches is considered the minimum width except on the roofs of canopies and small porches. If there is a screen or similar device to prevent anything but water from flowing into the gutter, its performance during a rainstorm should be checked to be sure water can actually enter the gutter. Check gutters without screens or similar devices to be sure that basket strainers are installed at each downspout.

Cleaning the gutters is a fun homeowner maintenance job.

Joints at the gutters should be soldered or sealed with mastic. Otherwise, they'll leak. The steeper the roof pitch, the lower the gutter should be placed or positioned. On roofs with lower slopes, gutters should be placed close to the roof's surface. Hangers should be placed no more than 3 feet apart. Where ice and snow are long-lasting, hangers should be placed no more than 18 inches apart. The strength of a gutter's fastening to the roof fascia or building exterior should be strong and secure. Rusted fasteners and missing hangers should be replaced.

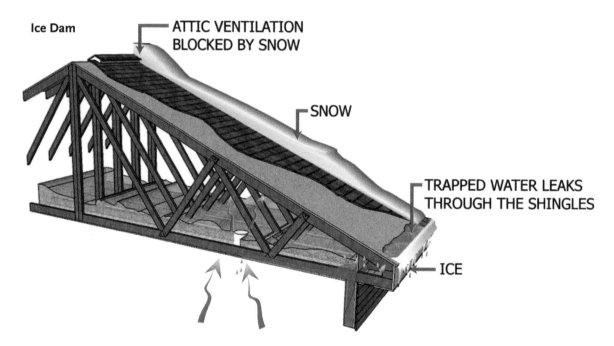

Ice Dam — ATTIC VENTILATION BLOCKED BY SNOW — SNOW — TRAPPED WATER LEAKS THROUGH THE SHINGLES — ICE

Ice dams. Ice dams can form on pitched-roof overhangs in cold climates subject to prolonged periods of freezing weather, especially those climates with a daily average January temperature of 30° F or less. Heat loss through the roof and heat from the sun (even in freezing temperatures) can cause snow on a roof to melt. As water runs down the roof onto the overhang, it freezes and forms an ice dam just above the gutter. The ice dam traps water from melting snow and forces it back under the shingles and into the building's interior.

Watch the edge of the roof overhang for evidence of ice dams and look at the eaves and soffit for evidence of deterioration and water damage. If the house has an attic, the underside of the roof deck at the exterior walls can be checked for signs of water intrusion.

Downspouts. The rule of thumb for downspouts is at least one downspout for every 40 feet of gutter. For roofs with gutters, make sure that downspouts discharge so water drains away from the foundation. Downspouts can be checked for size. Seven square inches is generally the minimum except for small roofs or canopies. There should be attachments or straps at the top, bottom, and at each intermediate joint.

Downspout fasteners can rust, deform, fail or become loose. On buildings with multiple roofs, one roof sometimes drains onto another roof. Where that happens, water should not discharge directly onto roofing material. The best practice is to direct water from higher gutters to discharge into lower gutters through downspout pipes.

Occasionally, wooden gutters and downspouts are used, usually in older and historic residences. They may be built into roof eaves and concealed by roof fascias. Wooden gutters are especially susceptible to rot and deterioration and should be monitored.

Pitched roofs in older buildings may end at a parapet wall with a built-in gutter integrated with the roof flashing. At this location, drainage is accomplished by a scupper, which is a metal-lined opening through the parapet wall that discharges into a leader head box that, in turn, discharges into a downspout.

The leader head box should have a strainer. Monitor the scupper for deterioration and open seams. All metal roof flashings, scuppers, leader head boxes and downspouts should be made of similar metals to prevent galvanic corrosion.

According to the Standards of Practice:

The inspector will inspect the roof covering from the ground or eaves, vents, flashing, skylights, chimney and other roof penetrations. The inspector is not required to walk on the roof, perform a water test, or warrant the roof. Skylights are notorious for developing leaks. Prediction of when, how or where a leak will develop is beyond the scope of a visual home inspection.

Chapter 4: Building Exterior

The exterior of your home is slowly deteriorating and aging. The sun, wind, rain and temperatures are constantly affecting it. Your job is to monitor the building's exterior for its condition and weathertightness.

Check the condition of all exterior materials and look for developing patterns of damage or deterioration.

In hurricane regions, examine screen and jalousie enclosures, carports, awnings, canopies, porch roofs and roof overhangs to determine their condition and the stability of their fastenings. Then, examine the following four critical areas of the exterior to determine their condition and strength: roofs; windows; doors; and garage doors.

In locations where wildfires can occur, some jurisdictions have restrictions on the use of flammable exterior materials. Check with the local building official or the fire marshal, or both, for detailed information.

Exterior House

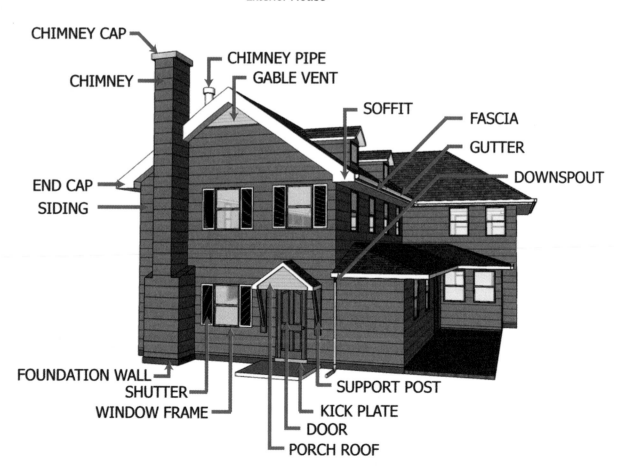

4.1 Foundation Walls and Piers

It is easy to walk around the house and simply check the exterior of the foundation and structural supports.

Foundation walls and piers in residential buildings are usually made of masonry and should be monitored for cracking, deterioration, moisture intrusion and structural adequacy.

Annual inspections are recommended as part of a regular home maintenance plan. Your home inspector can check the structural integrity of your home, including wooden posts, wooden columns, concrete foundations and piers.

4.2 Exterior Wall Covering

Exterior walls above the foundation may be covered with a variety of materials, including wood siding, aluminum, vinyl, asbestos cement shingles, plywood, stucco, brick, and stone masonry or an exterior insulation and finish system.

Exterior wooden components. Periodically look at all painted surfaces for peeling, blistering and checking. Paint-related problems may be due to vapor pressure beneath the paint, improper paint application, or excessive paint build-up. Corrective measures for these problems could vary from the installation of moisture vents to complete paint removal. Mildew stains on painted surfaces do not hurt the wood and could be cleaned with a mildew remover. All wood elements should be checked for fungal and insect infestation at exposed horizontal surfaces and exterior corner joints.

Clearance. Check the distance between the bottom of wood elements and grade. In locations that have little or no snow, the distance should be no less than 8 inches. In locations with significant lasting snow, the bottom of wood elements should be no less than 8 inches above the average snow depth. Do not pile up against the house wall landscaping materials, such as wood chips and mulch.

Aluminum and vinyl siding. Aluminum and vinyl siding are low-maintenance materials. When you are outside, you can easily look around and check the siding. Check for loose, bent, cracked or broken pieces. Seasonally, inspect all caulked joints, particularly around window and door trim. Many communities require aluminum siding to be electrically grounded. Your inspector can confirm proper grounding.

Asbestos cement shingles. Asbestos is a hazardous material. Asbestos is no longer used in building materials. Do no cut or sand asbestos siding. Dust containing asbestos fibers can be inhaled. Asbestos siding can be replaced with modern and safer siding material. Asbestos siding can be completely removed or covered over.

Siding Distance from Grade

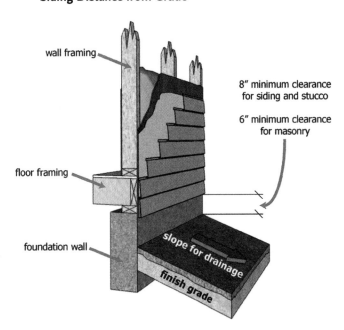

wall framing

8" minimum clearance for siding and stucco

6" minimum clearance for masonry

floor framing

foundation wall

slope for drainage

finish grade

Like aluminum and vinyl siding, asbestos cement shingles may cover decayed or insect-infested wood. Check for loose, cracked or broken pieces. Check around all window and door trim for signs of deterioration.

Stucco. Check stucco for cracks, crumbling sections and areas for potential water intrusion. Old and weathered cracks may be caused by the material's initial shrinkage or by earlier building settlement. New, sharp cracks may indicate movement behind the walls that should be investigated by a qualified professional. Stucco can be cleaned. It can also be painted.

Stucco: Three-Coat Process

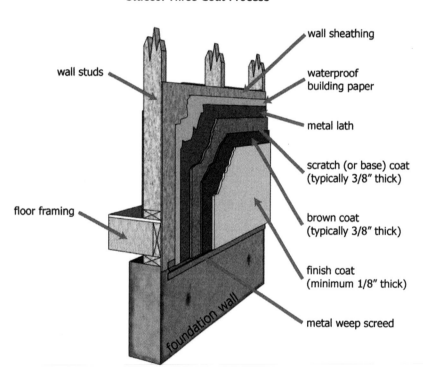

wall studs
floor framing
foundation wall

wall sheathing
waterproof building paper
metal lath
scratch (or base) coat (typically 3/8" thick)
brown coat (typically 3/8" thick)
finish coat (minimum 1/8" thick)
metal weep screed

Brick or stone veneers. Inspect veneers for cracking, mortar deterioration and spalling.

EIFS (exterior insulation and finish system). It generally consists of the following product layers (moving outward): insulation board, mesh and base coat layer, finish coat, and sealant and flashing. EIFS was originally designed as a non-draining water and moisture-barrier system. A drainage-type EIFS that allows water and moisture to penetrate the surface and then drain away has been developed more recently. Most existing EIFS in

residential applications is installed over wood framing and is of the non-draining type. Water leakage and consequent rotting of the wood framing have become serious problems in many installations, especially at wall openings, such as windows and doors, where inadequate flashing details can allow water seepage into the wall interior. Manufacturers of EIFS differ in their installation methods.

Inspecting existing EIFS is difficult because it is a proprietary product and there are no standard construction details that everyone agrees on. Consult a trained stucco inspector to check for concealed water/moisture intrusion and damage.

Insulation. Exterior walls of older homes may contain little or no thermal insulation. Examine behind the siding (when possible) to determine the presence of insulation, if any, and assess the potential for insulating the exterior walls. Ask your home inspector about thermal imaging and building evaluations.

Moisture. Check for signs of moisture problems. Where mildew and mold are evident on exterior cladding or where interior walls are damp, there is the possibility that condensation is occurring in the walls. Moisture problems generally occur in cold weather when outside temperatures and vapor pressures are low and there are a number of water vapor sources within the building. The presence of moisture may be a result of an improperly installed or failed vapor barrier, or no vapor barrier at all. If condensation is suspected, an analysis of the wall section in question should be made. This analysis will provide the information necessary to make the needed repairs.

4.3 Windows and Doors

Windows and doors are the most complex elements of your home's exterior and they require monitoring.

Exterior doors. Exterior doors should be checked often for their condition, operation, and functionality of their hardware. Door types include hinged, single and double doors of wood, steel, aluminum, and plastic with and without glazing. Monitor wood and plastic doors that are not protected from the weather. These doors should be rated for exterior use. In warm climates, jalousie doors may also be in use. Make sure the louvers close tightly for weathertightness. Some buildings use glass-framed doors of fixed and operable panels that have wood, vinyl-covered wood, and aluminum frames. Check the tracks of these sliding doors for dents, breaks and straightness.

Doors should also be monitored for the exterior condition of their frames and sills. Check doors that are not protected from the weather for the presence of essential flashing at the head. Over time, the interior condition and hardware of exterior doors can wear out or fail. In hurricane regions, exterior doors, and especially double doors, should have dead-bolt locks with a throw length of no less than 1 inch.

Windows. Window frames, sills and sashes should be monitored. The interior condition and hardware of windows change over time. In general, there are eight types of windows and six types of frame material in use in residential buildings. Frame materials include plastic, aluminum, steel, wood, plastic-clad wood and metal-clad (steel or aluminum) wood. Window types include double-hung, single-hung, casement, horizontal sliding, projected out or awning, projected in, and fixed. In addition to these, there are jalousies, which are glass louvers on an aluminum or steel frame.

At older sashes, the glazing compound or putty around glass panels should be monitored carefully, since this is a vulnerable part of the window and its repair is time-consuming.

Examine glazing tapes or strips around glass panels in steel or aluminum sashes for signs of deterioration, such as hardened sealant. Check metal sashes for weep holes that have been blocked by paint, sealant or dirt. Weep holes are usually easy to clean. In hurricane regions, check all windows and glass doors that are not protected by shutters to determine if they have been tested for impact resistance to windborne debris. If they have not been so tested, determine if plywood panels can be installed for their protection at the time of a hurricane warning.

Storm windows and doors should be monitored for operation, weathertightness, overall condition and fit. Check to see if paint, sealant, dirt or other substances have blocked any weep holes. Opening weep holes is usually easy to do. Blocked weep holes could cause wood rot and water intrusion at the window sill.

Weatherstripping. Window and door weatherstripping is generally one of three types: metal; foam plastic; or plastic stripping. Each type should have a good fit. Check the metal for dents, bends and straightness. Check foam plastic for resiliency, and plastic stripping for brittleness and cracks. Make sure the weatherstripping is securely held in place.

Shutters. Periodically check the shutters' operation and observe their condition and fit, and confirm the adequacy of the shutters for their purpose, including privacy, light control, security, and protection against bad weather. Window shutters are generally one of two types: decorative or functional. Decorative shutters are fixed to the exterior wall on either side of a window. Check the shutter's condition for change and pay attention to its mounting to the wall. Functional shutters are operable and can be used to close off a window.

Shutters close to the ground can be examined from the ground. Shutters out of reach from the ground should be examined from inside the house. In hurricane regions, check shutters to see if the shutter manufacturer has certified them for hurricane use. If they provide protection to windows and glass doors, determine if they have been tested for impact resistance to windborne debris.

Awnings. Monitor the condition of your awnings. The attachment to the exterior wall can become loose. Oftentimes, an attachment device in the mortar joint of a brick wall can be easily pulled or slid outward. Windows and glazed exterior doors sometimes have awnings over them, usually for sun control, but sometimes for decoration or protection from the weather. Awnings are usually made of metal, plastic, or fabric on a metal or plastic frame. Some are fixed in place, while others are operable and can be folded up against the exterior wall. If an awning can be used for sun control, its effect on energy conservation is typically a personal judgment.

Garage doors. Garage doors should be monitored for operation, weathertightness, overall condition and fit. Garage doors are made of wood, hardboard on a wood frame, steel, fiberglass on a steel frame, and aluminum. Garage doors come with glazed panes in a wide variety of styles. Wood and hardboard can rot, hardboard can crack and split, steel can rust, fiberglass can deteriorate from ultraviolet light, and aluminum can dent.

Doors with motors should be periodically tested using each of the operators on the system, such as key-lock switch or combination lock keypad, where control must be accessible on the exterior remote electrical switch, radio signal switch, or photo-electric control switch. Check the operation for smoothness, quietness, speed of operation, and safety. Check for the presence and proper operation of the door safety-reversing device. Look at the exposed parts of the installation for loose connections, rust, and bent or damaged pieces. In hurricane regions, make sure the garage door, especially single doors on two-car garage assemblies (door and track), have been tested for hurricane wind loads or have been reinforced.

4.4 Decks, Water and GFCIs

Decks, porches and balconies are exposed to the outside elements more than other parts of a home and, therefore, are more prone to deterioration.

Monitor the following:

Condition. Examine all porch, deck and balcony supports for components that may become loose or deteriorated. Masonry or concrete piers should remain plumb and stable. Structural connections to the building should remain secure and protected against corrosion and decay. Watch for signs of deflection and deterioration at porch and deck floors. Where the porch floor or deck is close to the level of the interior floor, watch for signs of water infiltration at the door sill. There should be a sufficient pitch of the porch floor or deck to direct water away from the exterior wall.

Exterior water. Exterior hose spigots should be frost-proof. You can't see the frost-proof feature from outside. Unlike a traditional hose bibb whose valve stem is an inch or 2 in length, the valve stem for a frost-proof hose bibb (or sillcock) could be 6 to 30 inches long. Thus, the valve is well within the exterior wall and protected from the cold and freezing.

GFCI. All exterior electrical receptacles should have GFCI protection.

4.5 Masonry and Metal Chimneys

Chimneys should project at least 2 feet above the highest part of a pitched roof and anything else that is within 10 feet. A chimney should project at least 3 feet from its penetration from the roof (required minimum heights may vary slightly). Flues should not be smaller in size than the discharge of the appliance they serve.

- Unlined chimneys are hazardous and they should be further evaluated by a chimney sweep.

- Flues should extend a minimum of 4 inches above the top of a masonry chimney.

- Masonry chimneys without hoods should have stone or reinforced concrete caps at the top. Some masonry chimneys have hoods over the flues. Hoods on masonry chimneys consist of stone or reinforced concrete caps supported on short masonry columns at the perimeter of chimney tops, or sheet metal caps supported on short sheet metal columns.

- If a cement wash or crown on top of the chimney is not properly sloped or is extensively cracked, spalled, or displays rust stains, it should be replaced. Reinforced concrete caps and stone caps with minor shallow spalling and cracking should be repaired. Those with extensive spalling or cracking should be replaced. Sheet metal hood caps with minor rust or corrosion should be repaired, but if rust or corrosion is extensive, replacement is needed.

- Metal spark screens are sometimes used on wood and coal-burning fireplace chimneys. Maintain the condition and fit of spark screens. Dirty or clogged screens adversely affect draft and could be a fire hazard.

- Where a masonry chimney is located on the side of a pitched roof, a cricket is needed on the higher side to divert water around the chimney. The cricket should extend the full width of the chimney.

- In seismic zones, there should be bracing of masonry chimneys from the top of the firebox to the cap, and particularly the portion projecting above the roof.

Pre-fab metal chimney. If the chimney is a prefabricated one encased in an exterior chase, the chase top should properly interlock with the metal chimney's counter-flashing so that the assembly is watertight. The chimney top should drain off water. There should be a rain cap on the top.

If the chimney is prefabricated metal and not encased, the adjustable flashing at the roof should be tightly sealed to the chimney, preferably with counter-flashing, and there should be a cap installed.

4.6 Lightning Protection

Lightning is a problem in some locations. You may want lightning protection for your home.

A lightning protection system consists of: lightning rods located on the roof and on projections, such as chimneys; main conductors that connect the lightning rods together and connect them with a grounding system; bonding to metal roof structures and equipment; arresters to prevent power-line surge damage; and ground terminals, which are usually rods or plates driven or buried in the earth. An electrician can install lightning surge protectors at the main electrical panelboard.

According to the Standards of Practice:

The inspector will inspect the siding, doors, decks and steps. The inspection should include a representative number of windows. The inspector is not required to inspect exterior components that are not visible or readily accessible from the ground. Interior chimney flues are beyond the scope of a home inspection. If your house has stucco, consider having the system inspected by a certified stucco inspector.

Chapter 5: Building Interior

 The most common problem that homeowners experience is water intrusion in the form of outside water penetration and plumbing leaks. Inside the house, always look for signs of water intrusion or material deterioration that may indicate underlying problems in the structural, electrical, plumbing or HVAC system. Consider hiring an inspector who is trained in the application of infrared thermography because thermal imaging is an excellent tool to use in the search for water intrusion.

5.1 Basement or Crawlspace

The basement or crawlspace is often the most revealing area in the home and usually provides a general picture of how the entire structure works. In most cases, the structure is exposed overhead, as are the HVAC distribution system, plumbing supply and DWV lines, and the electrical branch-circuit wiring.

Moisture Production from Domestic Activities

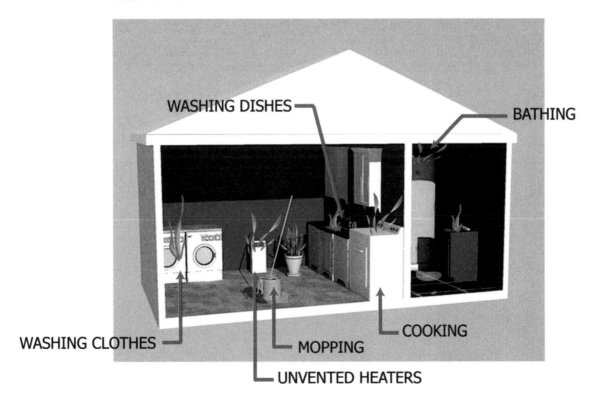

Moisture intrusion. One of the most common problems in small residential structures is a wet basement. You should monitor the walls and floors for signs of water penetration, such as dampness, water stains, peeling paint, efflorescence, and rust on exposed metal parts. In finished basements, look for rotted or warped wood paneling and doors, loose floor tiles, and mildew stains. It may come through the walls or cracks in the floor, or from backed-up floor drains, leaky plumbing lines, or a clogged air-conditioner condensate line.

To properly correct a moisture problem, you must determine the source of the moisture. There's no point in cleaning or wiping up a problem without investigating the source of the problem.

If moisture appears to be coming in through the walls, check the roof-drainage system and grading around the exterior of the building because the problem could be as simple as a clogged gutter. Check the sump pump, if there is one, to be sure its discharge is not draining back into the basement. Look for unprotected or poorly draining window wells, leaking exterior faucets, and signs of leakage in the water supply line near the building. Check the elevation of an earthen floor in a crawlspace. If the water table is high or the drainage outside the building is poor, the crawlspace floor should not be below the elevation of the exterior grade.

If the basement or crawlspace is merely damp or humid, the cause may simply be a lack of adequate ventilation. The ventilation could be checked by measurement and calculation, comparing the free area of vents with the floor area of the crawlspace. The ratio of free vent area-to-crawlspace should be 1 to 150 in a crawlspace with an earthen floor, and 1 to 1,500 in a crawlspace with a vapor barrier over the earthen floor. If the calculated ratio is less, consider adding ventilation, particularly in hot and humid climates, and especially if moisture is present. Check the location of the vents through the foundation or exterior wall. There should be one vent near every corner of the crawlspace to promote complete air movement. The vents should have screens with corrosion-resistant mesh.

Fungal and insect infestation. Always keep an eye out for signs of fungal growth, particularly in unventilated crawlspaces. Ask your home inspector to annually check all foundation walls, piers, columns, joists, beams and sill plates for signs of termites and other wood-destroying insects.

Thermal insulation. If you have access to the space above your unheated basement or crawlspace, examine the amount and type of insulating material installed, if any. Determine the amount of insulation that is recommended for the space, and whether additional insulation can or should be added. Check for an adequate vapor barrier. If you live in a cold climate, the vapor barrier should be installed on the warm interior-side of the wall. If you live in a warm climate, the vapor barrier should be installed on the exterior-side of the wall.

5.2 Interior Spaces

Monitor the following:

Walls and ceilings. Check the general condition of all surfaces and don't fret over cosmetic imperfections. Be aware of the signs of water intrusion into the building (including exterior water penetration and interior plumbing leaks). Look for cracks and peeling paint or wallpaper. Look for sags and bulges in plaster or drywall. Gently tap and push on areas of plaster; if an area sounds hollow or feels flexible, it is a good indication that the plaster has separated from its backing. If such areas are found, it may be best to re-plaster or overlay the wall or ceiling with wallboard.

Wall and ceiling cracks are usually caused by building settlement, deflection, warping of wood structural elements, or small seasonal movements of building components due to temperature and humidity variations. Seasonal movements will make some cracks regularly open and close; these may be filled with a flexible, paintable sealant, but otherwise cannot be effectively repaired. Cracks due to settlement, deflection or warping can be repaired if movement has stopped, as is often the case.

Large wall and ceiling cracks may indicate structural problems.

Nail pops. Homeowners often find nail popping, joint cracks, and other signs of minor cosmetic issues, such as rust stains at fasteners and corner beads.

You can check paneled walls by pushing or tapping on the paneling to determine if it is securely attached or has become loose in some way. Veneers can become delaminated. If the paneling is obviously not original to the house, try to look behind it to see what problems may be covered up.

Homeowners should lift suspended ceiling panels and look above them. Check the condition of the original ceiling, if one exists. Tiled ceilings should be examined similarly. On top floors, inspect for ceiling penetrations that may form thermal bypasses to the unconditioned spaces above.

Interior doors. Monitor the condition of doors and door frames, including the interior of entrance doors and storm doors. Check hardware for finish, wear and proper functioning. Sticking doors or out-of-square frames may indicate building settlement.

Windows. Look at the window sashes and frames for damage and deterioration. Check for a good fit and apparent weathertightness. When casement windows are open, they are easily damaged by wind, and hinge damage may keep them from closing properly. Casement hardware should operate smoothly and easily. Older double-hung windows may have old sash cords and weights that may break. Every once in a while, open windows above the ground floor and check their exterior surfaces, frames, sills, awnings and shutters, if any.

Safety glass. There are many areas in a house that require safety glass. These areas are hazardous because of their frequent impact by the home's occupants. Glazing installed in doors is of particular concern because of the increased probability of accidental impact while operating the doors. A person may often push against the glazed portion of a door in order to open it. A large piece of glass installed along a travel path where no barrier is provided is a potentially dangerous area. If the glass is safety glass, it will have a permanent label on it located in a corner.

Ventilation. Habitable rooms should be provided with operable windows. Their required opening size is a percentage of the floor area, usually 4%. A mechanical ventilation system can be provided in lieu of this requirement.

Egress. Basements and every sleeping room should have at least one operable emergency escape and rescue opening that opens directly into a public street, public alley, yard or court. Basements that have one or more sleeping rooms should have an emergency egress and rescue opening installed in each sleeping room, but this is not required for adjoining areas.

The sill height of the emergency escape and rescue opening should not be more than 44 inches above the floor.

Because many deaths and injuries happen when occupants are asleep at the time of a fire, this standard requires that basements and all sleeping rooms have doors or windows that can be used for rescue or escape in an emergency. During a fire, the normal means of escape will most likely be blocked.

If the emergency escape and rescue opening has a sill height below ground level, a window well should be provided. The window well should have a horizontal area of at least 9 square feet, with a minimum horizontal projection and width of 36 inches (with the exception of a ladder encroachment into the required dimension).

If an emergency escape window is located under a porch or deck, the porch or deck should allow the window to be fully opened and the escape path should be at least 3 feet in height.

Closets. Closets should have a clear depth of at least 24 inches. Watch out for an improperly installed light fixture. A closet needs the proper type and location for the light fixture. A light positioned close to a shelf presents a hazardous condition.

Electrical outlets and lighting. Generally speaking, each wall should have at least one wall outlet, and each room should have one switch-operated outlet or overhead light. When operating light switches, look for dimmed or flickering lights that may indicate electrical problems somewhere in the circuit. Also, check the light switches for sparks (arcing) when switches are turned on and off. Feel the light switches for overheating. Switches that are worn should be replaced. When a light does not turn on even after the bulb has been replaced, it will likely be the result of a bad switch.

HVAC source. For every room in the house, there should be a heating, cooling or ventilating source. If there is a warm-air supply register but no return, make sure the doors are undercut 1 inch for air flow.

Skylights. Monitor the undersides of all skylights for signs of leakage and water damage. Skylights are notorious for leaking water and causing water stains and damage.

Firewall. It is common for a fire to start in an attached garage. The fire may grow unnoticed by the occupants and become a significant hazard. Therefore, a minimum amount of fire protection is needed.

The door construction and fire rating of the door is important to know. The door between an attached garage and a home should be a solid wood door not less than 1-3/8 inches thick, a solid- or honeycomb-core steel door not less than 1-3/8 inches thick, or a 20-minute fire-rated door. In many jurisdictions, a self-closing device on the door may be required. The entire door assembly may have to be fire-rated.

A direct opening between an attached garage and a sleeping room is not permitted. That opening would be hazardous.

There should be at least ½-inch drywall (gypsum board) applied on the garage-side to separate the garage from the residence and its attic space. A garage located below a habitable room should be separated by at least 5/8-inch Type X drywall (gypsum board) or equivalent.

This standard requires a minimum level of fire protection from the garage to the home. It allows the occupants time to escape. The separation also restricts the spread of fire from the garage to the home until the fire can be controlled and extinguished.

5.3 Bathrooms

Plumbing. Obviously, you always want to check for water drips and leaks. Check the operation of the lavatory (sink), toilet, tub and shower. A common problem in bathrooms is water leakage around tubs and showers.

It is a good idea to look up and check the ceiling below each bathroom for signs of water or to spot the development of a major water leak.

If the toilet is not a water-saving fixture, consider replacing it with a water-saving toilet that has a 1.6-gallon flushing capacity. Pressure-assisted toilets use water pressure to compress air in a tank that makes the 1.5- to 1.6-gallon flush very effective in cleaning the fixture bowl and preventing buildup in the soil pipe.

Check the water traps for drips. Trap pipes made of older metal, such as soft brass with chrome coating, deteriorate and weaken over time.

Check the toilet for wobbling. If the toilet becomes loose and starts to wobble, a new wax seal may be needed.

A faulty shower pan may go undetected for decades until a major water leak develops. Monitor the ceiling below all showers for signs of water leakage.

Electrical. Wherever possible, switches and outlets should not be within arm's reach of the tub or shower. Ground-fault circuit interrupters (GFCIs) should be installed at the bathroom's electrical outlets. The GFCIs should be tested every month.

Tub and shower. Monitor the tub and shower enclosures. The glass or glazing should be safety glazing.

Ceramic tile. Push and pound on the tiles with your hand and check for loose tiles. Pull on the soap dish. Nothing should be loose or wiggly. Periodically watch for tiles that become damaged or loose, or tiles that become scratched, pitted or dulled by improper cleaning.

Monitor the condition of all grouted and caulked joints. If a portion of the tile is defective or missing, the tile may need to be replaced. Open cracks in the tile grout may allow water to penetrate behind the tile and cause damage.

Plumbing access panels. Open up the plumbing access panels every once in a while and check for developing water problems.

Ventilation. The bathroom should be ventilated by either a window or an exhaust fan. Poor ventilation will cause mildew to form on the ceiling and walls. If there is an exhaust fan, it should be properly ducted to exhaust to the outside.

5.4 Kitchen

Plumbing. All by themselves, plumbing connections could develop leaks. Check often for water drips and leaks in both the supply and drainage lines. When operating the disposal and dishwasher, listen and watch for smooth operation.

Counters and cabinets. Over time, cabinet doors and drawers can lose their smooth operation, and wall cabinets may become insecurely attached to the wall or other cabinets.

Electrical. All kitchen counter receptacles should be protected by ground-fault interrupters (GFCIs). Separate circuits

should be installed for each major appliance as follows: refrigerator 20 amp/120 volt; dishwasher 20 amp/120 volt; garbage disposal 20 amp/120 volt; range 40 to 50 amp/240 volt.

All electrical appliances should be able to operate simultaneously, including exhaust fans, and run steadily without overloading their circuits.

Ventilation. The kitchen exhaust fan and range hood should be ducted to the outside and not to a cupboard, attic, crawlspace or wall. A recirculation range hood fan is acceptable. Maintain and clean the filters. Ducts, hoods and filters should be free of grease buildup.

5.5 Storage Spaces

All closets and other storage spaces should be properly lit, ventilated, and kept clean to prevent vermin infestation.

5.6 Stairs and Hallways

Light. All interior and exterior stairways should have a means to illuminate the stairs, including landings and treads. Interior stairways should have a light located at each landing, except where a light is installed directly over each stairway section. Public stair and

hallway lights in multi-family buildings should be operated from centralized house controls.

Smoke detectors. Periodically check the operation of all smoke detectors by pushing their test buttons. Stairs and hallways are the appropriate locations for smoke detectors. They should be located on or near the ceiling, near the heads of stairs, and away from corners.

Current standards require a smoke detector in each sleeping room and in hallways adjacent to the sleeping rooms.

Structural integrity of stairs. All stairs must be kept structurally sound. Examine basement stairs where they meet the floor and where they are attached to the floor joists above.

Stair handrails and guardrails. You can check a railing's stability and its fastenings by shaking it vigorously. Handrails are normally required

to be 34 to 38 inches above the stair nosing on at least one side of all stairs with three or more risers. Guardrails are required on open sides of stairways and should have intermediate rails that do not allow the passage of a sphere 4 inches in diameter.

Stair treads and risers. All treads should be level and secure. Riser heights and tread depths should be as uniform as possible. As a guide, stairs in new residential buildings must have a maximum riser of 7-3/4 inches and a minimum tread of 10 inches.

Stair width and clearance. Stairs should normally have a minimum headroom of 6 feet and 8 inches and width of 3 feet.

5.7 Laundry and Utility Rooms

Laundry room. Watch for leaks and kinks developing at plumbing connections to the washer. Protect the electrical or natural gas connections to the dryer. Inspect dryer venting, and make sure it exhausts to the outside and is not clogged or restricted. A gas dryer vent that passes through walls or combustible materials must be made of metal.

Clothes dryer exhaust. A clothes dryer exhaust poses a different problem than other exhaust systems because the air is moist and carries lint. The exhaust of a dryer must vent outside and not discharge into an attic or crawlspace because the wooden structural members could be affected. Exhaust vents should have a backdraft damper installed to prevent cold air, rain, snow, rodents and pests from entering the vent.

The length of a clothes dryer exhaust ensures that the dryer exhaust blower will be able to push sufficient air volume to take away the moist air and lint. The length can be increased only when the make and model of the dryer is known, or when an approved blower-fan calculation is provided.

The maximum length of a clothes dryer exhaust duct should not be greater than 25 feet from the dryer location to the wall or roof termination. For each 45-degree bend, the maximum length

Dryer Exhaust

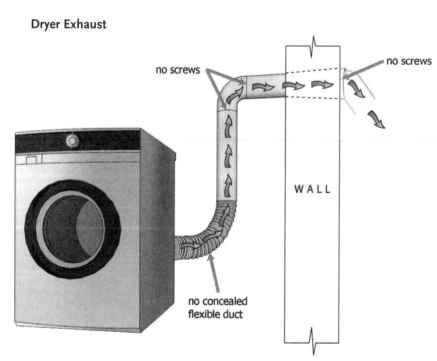

no screws

no screws

WALL

no concealed
flexible duct

of the duct is reduced by 2-1/2 feet. For each 90-degree bend, the maximum is reduced by 5 feet.

The maximum length of the exhaust duct does not include the transition duct.

Screens are not permitted on the clothes dryer exhaust vent because they can trap lint and debris and pose a fire hazard.

5.8 Fireplaces and Flues

Fireplaces. Each fireplace and flue in a house should be inspected by a certified chimney sweep every year. To find a sweep, visit **www.nachi.org/go/csia**

Every time prior to starting a fire, check the firebox for deterioration or damage. If there is a damper, check its operation. Make sure you open the damper prior to starting a fire! If smoke starts to billow out from the fireplace, the damper is closed or there is a major blockage in the flue.

Hearth. The hearth should be of adequate size to protect adjacent combustible building materials. For older fireplaces, the minimum depth from the face of the fireplace is 20 inches with a width that extends 1 foot beyond the fireplace opening on either side.

Flues. The flue lining in a masonry chimney should be inspected by a professional every year. It could be checked by your HVAC technician or a certified chimney sweep. The flue should be tight along its entire length. Linings should be intact, unobstructed and appropriate for the fuel type. An obstructed flue can usually be opened by a chimney sweep, but consult a chimney expert if the integrity of the flue is in doubt. Unlined chimneys should be updated with the installation of metal liners.

Furnace room. Rooms containing fuel-burning equipment should not be located off a sleeping room in a single-family residence and must be in a publicly accessible area in a multi-family building. Check local code requirements for applicable fire safety and combustion air criteria.

Chimney Deterioration Due to Condensation

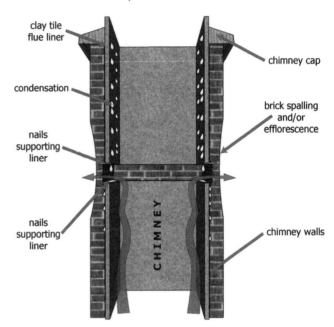

Smoke pipe connections. Every once in a while, check that the smoke pipes from furnaces, water heaters, stoves, and related devices are tightly connected to the chimney.

Ash dump and pit. If the fireplace has an ash dump at the bottom of the firebox, check the operation, fit and condition of the door, and check the shaft to the ash pit to be certain it is unobstructed and not overflowing with ashes. If the chimney has an ash pit, check the operation, fit and condition of the pit access door. The fit should be tight enough to prevent dust and ash from escaping. Cleaning the ashes is part of regular maintenance of the fireplace.

5.9 Attics, Roof Trusses and Vents

An attic is defined here as an unconditioned space between the roof and the ceiling or walls of the building's inhabited rooms. In small residential buildings with pitched roofs, attics are usually partially or fully accessible. In buildings with low-slope roofs, they may be inaccessible or virtually nonexistent.

Roof leaks. Look for signs of and monitor water leakage from the roof above and try to locate the source. This may be difficult to do beneath built-up roofs or beneath loosely laid and mechanically fastened single-ply roofs, since water may travel horizontally between layers of roofing materials.

Attic ventilation. Signs of inadequate ventilation are rusting nails (in roof sheathing, soffits, and drywall ceilings), wet or rotted roof sheathing, and excessive heat buildup in attics. Adequate attic ventilation can be measured by calculating the ratio of the free area of all vents to the floor area. The free area of vents is defined as their clear, open area. If a vent has an insect screen, its free area is reduced by half. The free vent area-to-floor area ratio should be 1 to 150. If the calculated ratio is less, consider adding ventilation, especially in hot and humid climates.

When an attic also contains an occupied space, check that the ventilation from the unconditioned, unoccupied areas at the eaves is continuous to the gable or ridge vents. Also check that the free area of eave vents is approximately equal to the free area of ridge or gable vents. If ventilation appears to be inadequate and additional vents cannot be added economically, consider adding mechanical ventilation.

Rafter space ventilation. Most homes with low-slope roofs and some with pitched roofs do not have attics. Instead, these structures have ceilings at the bottom of joists, rafters or trusses. The truss space and the space between each joist or rafter and above the ceiling need ventilation. At ridge, cornice, eave or soffit vents, install insect screens.

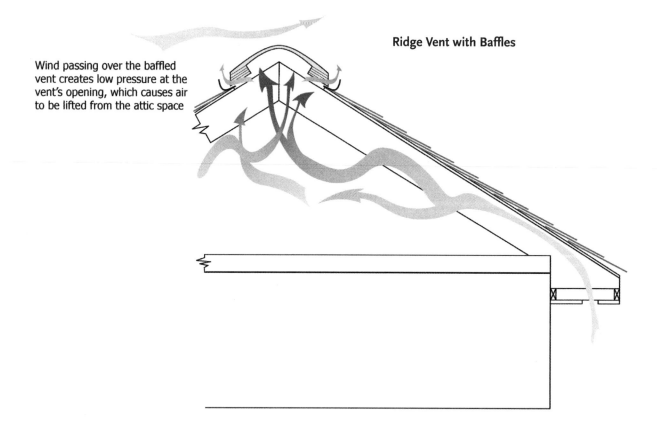

Ridge Vent with Baffles

Wind passing over the baffled vent creates low pressure at the vent's opening, which causes air to be lifted from the attic space

Vents and birds. Make sure ventilation openings are clear of dirt and debris. At larger ventilation openings on a building's exterior and where louvered grilles are used, such as at gables, check for the presence of 1-½-inch-square 14- or 16-gauge aluminum mesh bird screen. If there is none or it is in poor condition, consider having new bird screen installed.

Thermal insulation. Every homeowner should know the amount and type of insulating material installed in the house. For cold climate zones, the insulation faced with a vapor barrier should be installed face-side down with the vapor barrier closest to the conditioned space. The vapor barrier should be properly located between the ceiling and the first layer of insulation.

Determine the proper amount of insulation to the attic and whether additional insulation is needed. If attic insulation is placed against the roof sheathing, a ventilated air space between the insulation and the sheathing will be needed. If there is no air space, check for the presence of moisture and deterioration of the sheathing or rafters.

Ensure that insulation is held away from recessed lighting fixtures, and look at the spaces around vents, stacks, ducts and wiring for thermal bypasses. Inspect attic doors or access hatches, heating or cooling ducts that pass through the attic, and whole-house attic fans for thermal bypasses. Check the local jurisdiction for thermal resistance (R-value) requirements.

Plumbing stacks and exhaust ducts. All plumbing stacks should continue through the roof and should not terminate in the attic. The stack pipes should not be loose, broken or damaged. Exhaust ducts should not be kinked, broken or damaged and should not terminate in the attic but either continue through the roof, gable or wall.

5.10 Whole-Building Thermal-Efficiency Tests

Several whole-building tests can be performed to help evaluate the thermal efficiency of the building envelope. Ask your home inspector about performing a Home Energy Inspection or assessment on your home.

A building-pressurization test can be used to determine the rate of air infiltration and exfiltration. The test is particularly useful for "tightening up" an older building. A tracer gas test may also be used.

A hand-held infrared camera can be used to detect building "hot spots" due to interior air leakage or excessive heat loss through un-insulated building components. This test could be performed in cold weather when the building is heated. The greater the differential between the inside and outside temperatures, the more accurate the results. Thermography inspections should be performed by an energy specialist, certified home inspector, or others with the proper training and equipment.

5.11 Sound Transmission

The floors and walls between dwelling units should have adequate sound-transmission control using the current building code for guidance. Walls and floors that separate dwelling units in two-family residences, and walls that separate townhouses, should have an adequate sound-transmission control.

5.12 Asbestos

Asbestos is a naturally occurring fibrous mineral used in many construction products. It is considered to be a carcinogen. Asbestos has been used in: sealant, putty, and spackling compounds; in vinyl floor tiles, backing for vinyl sheet flooring, and flooring adhesives; in ceiling tiles; in textured paint; in exterior wall and ceiling insulation; in roofing shingles; in cement board for many uses, including siding; in door gaskets for furnaces and wood-burning stoves; in concrete piping; in paper, mill board and cement board sheets used to protect walls and floors around wood-burning stoves; in fabric connectors between pieces of metal ductwork; in hot water and steam piping insulation, blanket covering and tape; and as insulation on boilers, oil-fired furnaces and coal-fired furnaces. The use of asbestos was phased out in 1978, but many older houses contain asbestos-bearing products.

Products containing asbestos are not always a health hazard. The potential health risk occurs when these products become worn or deteriorate in a way that releases asbestos fibers into the air. Of particular concern are those asbestos-containing products that are soft, that were sprayed or troweled on, or that have become crumbly.

The Environmental Protection Agency believes that as long as the asbestos-bearing product is intact, is not likely to be disturbed, and is in an area where repairs or rehabilitation will not occur, it is best to leave the product in place. If it is deteriorated, it may be enclosed, coated or sealed up (encapsulated) in place, depending upon the degree of deterioration. Otherwise, it should be removed by a professional.

A certified environmental professional could perform an inspection and make the decision whether to enclose, coat, encapsulate or remove deteriorated asbestos-containing products. Testing by a qualified laboratory, as directed by the environmental professional, may be needed in order to make an informed decision. Encapsulation, removal and disposal of asbestos products must be done by a qualified asbestos-abatement contractor.

For more information, visit **www.nachi.org/go/epaasbestos**

5.13 Lead

Lead has been determined to be a significant health hazard if ingested, especially by children. Lead damages the brain and nervous system, adversely affects behavior and learning, slows growth, and causes problems related to hearing, pregnancy, high blood pressure, the nervous system, memory and concentration.

Lead-based paint. Most homes in the U.S. built before 1940 used paint that was heavily leaded. No more than half the homes built between 1940 and 1960 are believed to contain heavily leaded paint. In the period from 1960 to 1980, fewer homes used lead-based paint. In 1978, the U.S. Consumer Product Safety Commission (CPSC) set the legal limit of lead in most types of paint to a trace amount. As a result, homes built after 1978 should be nearly free of lead-based paint. In 1996, the U.S. Congress passed the final phase of the Residential Lead-Based Paint Hazard Reduction Act, Title X, which mandates that real estate agents, sellers and landlords disclose the known presence of lead-based paint in homes built prior to 1978.

Lead in paint. Lead-based paint that is in good condition and out of the reach of children is usually not a hazard. Peeling, chipping, chalking or cracking lead-based paint is a hazard and needs immediate attention.

Lead-based paint may be a hazard when found on surfaces that children can chew or that get a lot of wear and tear, such as windows and window sills, doors and door frames, stairs, railings, banisters, porches and fences. Lead from paint chips that are visible and lead dust that is not always visible can both be serious hazards. Lead dust can form when lead-based paint is dry-scraped, dry-sanded or heated. Dust also forms when painted surfaces bump or rub together, such as when windows open and close. Lead chips and dust can get on surfaces and objects that people touch. Settled lead dust can re-enter the air when people vacuum, sweep or walk through it.

If the building is thought to contain lead-based paint, consider having a qualified professional check it for lead hazards. This is done by means of a paint inspection that will identify the lead content of every painted surface in the building and a risk assessment that will determine whether there are any sources of serious lead exposure (such as peeling paint and lead dust). The risk assessment will also identify actions to take to address these hazards. The U.S. federal government has standards for inspectors and risk assessors. Some states may have standards in place. Call local authorities for help with locating qualified local professionals. Do-it-yourself home tests should not be the only method used before doing rehabilitation or to ensure safety. For more information on lead-based

paint, consult the HUD Office of Lead Hazard Control website at www.nachi.org/go/epalead

Lead in water. Lead in drinking water is a direct result of lead that is part of the plumbing system itself. Lead solder was used in pipe fittings in houses constructed prior to 1988. Lead has been used in plumbing fixtures, such as faucets, and in some older homes, the service water pipe from the main in the street to the house is made of lead. The transfer of lead into water is determined primarily by exposure (the length of time that water is in contact with lead). Two other factors that affect the transfer are water temperature (hot water dissolves lead quicker than cold water) and water acidity ("soft" water is slightly corrosive and reacts with lead). The current federal standard for lead in water is a limit of 15 parts per billion. The only way to find out whether there is lead in the house's water is to have the water tested by an approved laboratory. If there is evidence of lead in the system, consider having water tested for lead. If the house has a water filter, check to see if it is certified to remove lead.

For more information on lead in drinking water, call the Environmental Protection Agency's Safe Drinking Water Hotline at 800-462-4791 or visit the website of the EPA Office of Water at www.nachi.org/go/epasafewater

5.14 Radon Gas

Radon is a colorless, odorless and tasteless gas that is present in varying amounts in the ground and in water. Radon is produced by the natural radioactive decay of uranium deposits in the earth. Prolonged exposure to radon in high concentrations can cause cancer. The EPA has set guidelines for radon levels in residential buildings.

Airborne radon. The EPA recommends that mitigation measures be undertaken in residential buildings when radon concentrations are 4 picoCuries per liter (4 pCi/L) of air and above.

The radon concentration in a house varies with time and is affected by the uranium-radium content in the soil, the geological formation beneath the house, the construction of the house, rain, snow, barometric pressure, wind, and pressure variations caused by the periodic operation of exhaust fans, heating systems, fireplaces, attic fans and range fans. Radon concentrations are variable and may be high in one house and low in an adjacent house. To determine if a house has a radon problem, it must be tested.

A long-term test is the most accurate method of determining the average annual radon concentration. However, because time is usually limited, there are short-term tests that have a testing period of three to seven days. Radon tests are available from most home hardware stores or through radon testing service companies.

Radon in water. A house's domestic water supply from its well can contain radon. There are locations with well water containing 40,000 pCi/L or more. The health problems from drinking water with radon are insignificant compared to breathing airborne radon, but radon can be released into the air when water is run into a plumbing fixture or during a shower. It takes a high concentration of radon in water to produce a significant concentration in the large volume of air in a house.

Private well water testing is normally not a part of radon testing. Therefore, if the house has a private well, consult the local health department to determine whether water testing in the house's area is recommended.

Annual testing of the water quality of a private well is considered part of a regular home maintenance plan. Many home inspectors perform water quality sampling.

If a building is found to have a radon problem, consult a certified radon mitigation contractor. For more information on radon, visit **www.nachi.org/go/eparadonpubs**

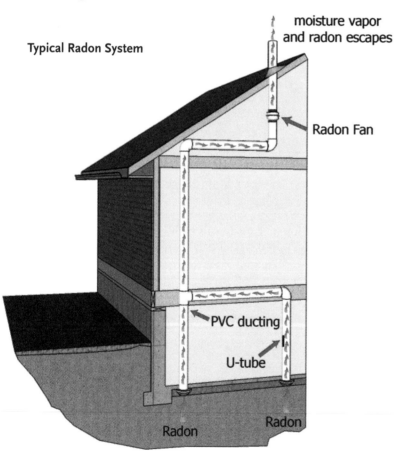

Typical Radon System

moisture vapor and radon escapes

Radon Fan

PVC ducting

U-tube

Radon

Radon

5.15 Tornado Safe Room

If a building is located in a tornado-risk area, it should have a tornado shelter or safe room, and it should be structurally adequate.

According to the Standards of Practice:

At the fireplace, the inspector should open and close the damper, check the hearth, and report major deficiencies. The inspector is not required to inspect the flue or vent system. Inspectors do not operate inserts or ignite pilot flames. The inspector is not required to operate any appliances. Environmental hazards, such as lead and radon, are beyond the scope of a general home inspection.

The inspector should flush toilets and run water at all the plumbing fixtures. The inspector should report any present conditions or clear indications of active water penetration he/she observes. Predicting water intrusion from either groundwater or the plumbing system is beyond the scope of a home inspection.

Chapter 6: Structural System

Most homes do not have major structural problems, but some do. In a well-maintained, modern residential building, there may be no major structural problems. Homes built in the 19th century often show signs of settlement and may have only minor structural faults that can be readily remedied. Major structural problems, when they do develop, are usually quite obvious. It is the less obvious problems that require careful inspection and informed diagnosis. Such problems are often detected through a pattern of symptoms rather than by any singular symptom.

The following information describes signs of structural distress, deterioration and damage by material type, including masonry (the most difficult to assess), wood, iron, steel and concrete.

Assessing structural capacity. A thorough visual home inspection of the structural components is all that is normally necessary to verify the home's structural design and its structural integrity. Unless there is obvious overloading, significant deterioration of important structural components, or additional loading is anticipated, there is usually little need for evaluation by an engineer.

If the building's structural loading will be dramatically increased by things such as a new water bed, installation of a stone kitchen countertop, tile flooring, or heavy stove and oven, a quantitative analysis should be made of all the structural members involved. Simple calculations may be made or the local building code may be sufficient. More complex calculations could be performed by a qualified structural engineer.

6.1 Seismic Resistance

If the building is in seismic zones 2B, 3 or 4 (California, Idaho, Nevada, Oregon, Washington, and portions of Alaska, Arizona, Arkansas, Hawaii, Missouri, Montana, New Mexico, Utah and Wyoming), have a structural engineer check the following conditions for structural vulnerability. (Note that wood frame buildings with brick or stone veneer are still considered wood frame.)

- wood frame buildings that are not physically anchored to their foundations. Such buildings may be vulnerable to shifting or sliding;

- wood frame buildings and wood-framed portions, including porches, and other buildings that are supported above ground on either short wood studs (cripple walls) or on piers of stone, masonry or concrete. Such buildings may be vulnerable to tilting or falling over;

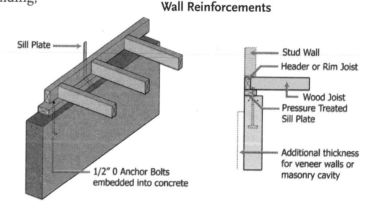

Wall Reinforcements

Sill Plate

1/2" 0 Anchor Bolts embedded into concrete

Stud Wall
Header or Rim Joist
Wood Joist
Pressure Treated Sill Plate
Additional thickness for veneer walls or masonry cavity

- un-reinforced and inadequately reinforced masonry buildings. Such buildings may be vulnerable to total or partial collapse due to inadequate reinforcement or to inadequate anchorage of roofs and walls to the floors;

- buildings of any type that have irregular shapes. Such buildings may be vulnerable to partial collapse;

- wood frame and masonry buildings with more than one story above grade whose story at grade is a large, unobstructed open space, such as a garage. Such buildings may be vulnerable to collapse of the story at grade; and

- wood frame and masonry buildings with more than one story above grade that are constructed on sloping hillsides, and buildings of any type of construction and height that are constructed on steep slopes of 20 degrees or more. Such buildings may be vulnerable to sliding.

If the building is in seismic zone 2A (Connecticut, Massachusetts, Rhode Island, South Carolina, and portions of Georgia, Illinois, Indiana, Kansas, Kentucky, Maine, New Hampshire, New Jersey, New York, North Carolina, Oklahoma, Pennsylvania, Tennessee, Vermont and Virginia) and has more than two stories above grade, consider having a structural engineer check for the previous two conditions (large, unobstructed open space at grade and sloped sites).

Buildings not of wood frame or masonry construction (such as stone, adobe, log, and post-and-beam structures), as well as buildings with more than one type of construction in any seismic zone, should be investigated by a structural engineer to determine their seismic vulnerability.

Masonry bearing-wall buildings in seismic zones 2B, 3 and 4 should be investigated by a structural engineer for the presence of reinforcing steel.

Have a structural engineer check the anchorage of wood frame structures to their foundations and investigate all such structures supported on cripple walls or piers in seismic zones 2, 3 and 4.

In all seismic zones, a structural engineer should investigate buildings with more than one story above grade whose story at grade is a large, unobstructed open space, or the building is on a sloping hillside and in seismic zones 2B, 3 and, 4, and buildings with an irregular shape.

6.2 Wind Resistance

Hurricanes are large, slow-moving, damaging storms characterized by gusting winds from different directions, rain, flooding, high waves and storm surges. The coasts of the Gulf of Mexico, the south- and mid-Atlantic coast, the coastal areas of Puerto Rico and the U.S. Virgin Islands and Hawaii, as well as the U.S. territories of American Samoa and Guam, are vulnerable to hurricanes in the late summer and early fall. Winter storms along the mid- and north-Atlantic coast can be more damaging than hurricanes because of their greater frequency, longer duration, and high-erosion impacts on the coastline. Even in states not normally considered susceptible to extreme windstorms, there are areas that experience dangerously high winds. These areas are typically near mountain ranges and include the Pacific Northwest coast. Other extreme-wind areas include the Plains states, which are especially subject to tornadoes.

In addition to the direct effects of high winds and winter on buildings, hurricanes and other severe storms generate airborne debris that can damage buildings.

Debris. Debris, such as small stones, tree branches, roof shingles and tiles, building parts and other objects, is picked up by the wind and moved with enough force to damage and even penetrate windows, doors, walls and roofs. When a building's exterior envelope is breached by debris, the building can become pressurized, subjecting its walls and roof to much higher damaging wind pressures. In general, the stronger the wind, the larger and heavier the debris it can carry and the greater the risk of severe damage.

If the building is in a hurricane or high-wind

region, consider having a structural engineer check its structural system for continuity of load path, including resistance to uplift forces. If there is an accessible attic, improper attachment of the roof sheathing to the roof-framing members can be checked by looking for unengaged or partially engaged nails.

Hurricane hold-down clips for joists, rafters and trusses should be present at the exterior walls. Examine the gable end walls and the roof trusses for lateral bracing. Check to see whether the exterior wall and other load-bearing walls are securely attached to the foundation.

6.3 Masonry

A homeowner should know which walls are load-bearing and which are not. Usually, this can be understood by examining the beams and joists in the building's basement, crawlspace and/or attic. All exposed masonry should be monitored for cracking, spalling, bowing (vertical bulges), sweeping (horizontal bulges), leaning, and mortar deterioration.

Masonry cracking. Monitoring the masonry walls of the house is needed. Although masonry can deform elastically over long periods of time to accommodate small amounts of movement, large movements normally cause cracking. Cracks may appear along the mortar joints or through the masonry units. Cracking can result from a variety of problems: differential settlement of the foundation; drying shrinkage (particularly in concrete block); expansion and contraction due to ambient thermal and moisture variations; improper support over openings; the effects of freeze-thaw cycles; the corrosion of iron and steel wall reinforcement; differential movement between building materials; expansion of salts; and the bulging or leaning of walls.

Cracks in Foundation

horizontal crack high on wall

foundation pushed inward

foundation crack low on wall

foundation pushed inward

concrete floor pushed upward

Cracks should always be further evaluated to determine their cause and whether corrective action is required.

Look for signs of movement. A clean crack indicates recent movement; a dirty or previously filled crack may be inactive. Correlate the width of larger cracks to the age of the building. A ½-inch crack in a new building may be a sign of rapid settlement, but in a building 50 years old, it may indicate a very slow movement of only 1/100 of an inch per year.

Crack movement can be measured with a commercially available joint-movement indicator. This device is temporarily fastened over the crack and a scribe records movement over a period of time.

Cyclical. Cyclical movements may take six months or more to measure, but diurnal movements can be recorded over a few days. Cracks associated with thermal expansion and contraction may open and close with the seasons. These are cyclical cracks, which may gradually expand as accumulating mortar debris jams them farther apart after each cycle. Such cracks should be cleaned and protected by flexible sealants. Re-pointing cyclical cracks will hold them open and cause more cracking.

When there are major masonry problems, it is advisable to consult a structural engineer. If problems appear to be due to differential settlement, a soil engineer may also be required.

Mortar deterioration. The age of the building is a good clue in evaluating its mortar problems. The two important qualities of mortar are its ability to bond to masonry and its internal strength. Older mortar (or mortar of any age that uses hydrated lime) is softer and may require re-pointing.

Moisture. Most often, mortar deterioration is found in areas of excessive moisture, such as near leaking downspouts, below windows, and at the tops of walls. In such cases, the remedy is to redirect the water flow and re-point the mortar joints. Re-pointing should be performed with mortar of a composition similar to or compatible with the original mortar. The use of high-strength mortar to repair mortar of a lower strength can do serious damage to the masonry because the pointing can't flex with the rest of the joint.

It is useful to remember that mortar acts as a drainage system to equalize hydrostatic pressure within the masonry. Nothing should be done to reduce its porosity and thereby block water flow to the exterior surface.

Deterioration of brick masonry units. The spalling, dusting or flaking of brick masonry units may be due to either mechanical or chemical damage. Mechanical damage is caused by moisture entering the brick and freezing, resulting in spalling of the brick's outer layers. Spalling may continue or may stop on its own after the outer layers that trapped the interior moisture have broken off. Chemical damage is due to the leaching of chemicals from the ground into the brick, resulting in internal deterioration. External signs of such deterioration are a dusting or flaking of the brick. Very little can be done to correct existing mechanical and chemical damage except for actually replacing the brick. Mechanical deterioration can be slowed or stopped by directing water away from the masonry surface and by re-pointing mortar joints to slow water entry into the wall.

Damage to Masonry Wall Caused by Rising Moisture

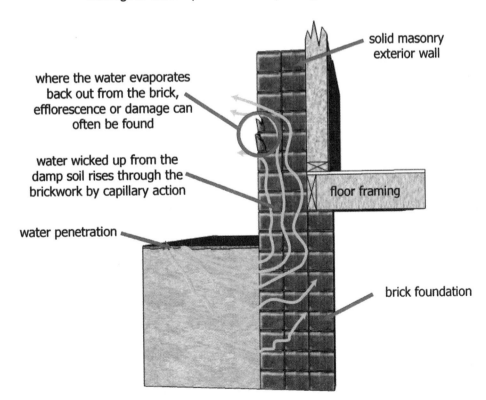

where the water evaporates back out from the brick, efflorescence or damage can often be found

water wicked up from the damp soil rises through the brickwork by capillary action

water penetration

solid masonry exterior wall

floor framing

brick foundation

6.4 Masonry Foundation and Piers

At the foundation walls (stone, brick, concrete, or concrete block), look for the following problems:

Uneven settlement. Uneven or differential settlement can be a major structural problem in small residential buildings. Serious settlement problems are relatively uncommon. Many signs of masonry distress are incorrectly diagnosed as settlement-related when, in fact, they are due to moisture and thermal movements.

Indications of differential settlement include vertical distortion or cracking of masonry walls, warped interior and exterior openings, sloped floors, and sticking doors and windows. Settlement most often occurs early in the life of a building or when there is a dramatic change in underground conditions. Often, such settlement is associated with improper foundation design, particularly inadequate footers and foundation walls.

- changes in water table level;

- soil erosion around footers from poor surface drainage, faulty drains, leaking water mains or other underground water movement (occasionally, underground water may scour away earth along only one side of a footer, causing its rotation and the subsequent buckling or displacement of the foundation wall above); and

- soil compaction or movement due to vibration from heavy equipment, vehicular traffic, or blasting, or from ground tremors (earthquakes).

Gradual differential settlement over a long period of time may produce no masonry cracking at all, particularly in walls with older and softer bricks and high lime mortars; the wall will elastically deform instead. More rapid settlement, however, produces cracks that taper, being largest at one end and diminishing to a hairline at the other, depending on the direction and location of settlement below the wall.

Soil Pressure on Foundation

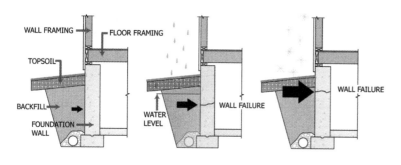

WALL FRAMING — FLOOR FRAMING
TOPSOIL
BACKFILL
FOUNDATION WALL
WATER LEVEL
WALL FAILURE
WALL FAILURE

DRY SOIL
- EXERTS A FORCE AGAINST THE FOUNDATION

WET SOIL
- EXERTS A GREATER FORCE AGAINST THE FOUNDATION THAN DRY SOIL

FROZEN SOIL
- EXERTS A GREATER FORCE AGAINST THE FOUNDATION THAN WET SOIL

Cracking is most likely to occur at corners and adjacent to openings, and usually follows a rough diagonal along mortar joints (although individual masonry units may be split). Settlement cracks (as opposed to the similar-appearing shrinkage cracks that are especially prevalent in concrete block) may extend through contiguous building elements, such as floor slabs, masonry walls above the foundation, and interior plaster work.

Other causes of settlement are:

- soil consolidation under the footings;

- soil shrinkage due to the loss of moisture to nearby trees or large plants;

- soil swelling due to inadequate or blocked surface or house drainage;

- soil heaving due to frost or excessive root growth;

- gradual downward drift of clay soils on slopes;

Tapering cracks, or cracks that are nearly vertical and whose edges do not line up, may occur at the joints of projecting bay windows, porches and additions. These cracks indicate differential settlement due to inadequate foundations or piers under the projecting element. Often, settlement slows a short time after construction and an equilibrium is reached during which movement no longer occurs.

Minor settlement cracking is structurally harmful only if long-term moisture leakage through the cracks adversely affects building elements. Large differential settlements, particularly between foundation walls and interior columns or piers, are more serious because they will cause movement in contiguous structural elements, such as beams, joists, floors and roofs that must be evaluated for loss of bearing and, occasionally, fracture.

Repair. If the foundation needs repair, it can be accomplished by the addition of new structural elements, such as pilasters, or by pressure-injecting concrete epoxy grout into the foundation wall. If movement continues and cracking is extensive, it is possible that the problem can only be rectified by underpinning. Older buildings with severe settlement problems may be very costly to repair.

Masonry piers. Masonry piers are often used to support internal loads on small residential buildings and to support projecting building elements, such as bay windows, porches, decks and additions. In some cases, they support the entire structure. Piers often settle differentially, and over a long period of time (particularly when they are exposed to the weather), they tend to deteriorate.

Structural Failure

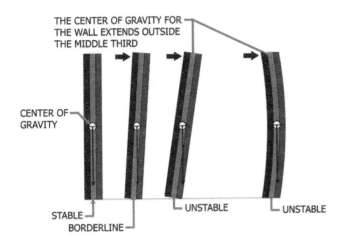

What to look for:

- Piers should be plumb, without major settlement, in good condition, and adequate in accepting bearing loads. Their width-to-height ratio should not exceed 1:10. Those that are deficient should be repaired or replaced. When appearance is not a factor (as is often the case), piers can be supplemented by the addition of adjacent supports.

- Settlement or rotation of the pier footing can cause a lowering or tilting of the pier and subsequent loss of bearing capacity. Wood frame structures adjust to this condition by flexing and redistributing their loads or by sagging. Masonry walls located over settled piers will crack.

- Frost heaving of the footing or pier, a condition caused by the lack of an adequate footing or one of insufficient depth, can raise or tilt a pier. This could show up as movement similar to that caused by settlement or rotation of the footing. Such a condition is most common under porches and decks.

- Above-ground piers exposed to the weather are subject to freeze-thaw cycles and subsequent physical damage. Deterioration of the pier could be caused by exposure, poor construction, or over-stressing. Piers for many older residential structures are often of poorly constructed masonry that deteriorates over the years. A sign of over-stressing of piers is vertical cracking or bulging.

- Problems with piers can result in problems with bearing of wooden components. Structural wooden components can lose bearing strength when piers move or deteriorate.

- Cracking can form from the drying shrinkage in concrete block foundation walls. The shrinkage of concrete block walls as they dry in place often results in patterns of cracking similar to that caused by differential settlement, including tapering cracks that widen as they move diagonally upward. These cracks usually form during the building's first year, and in existing buildings will appear as old cracks and exhibit no further movement. Although such cracks are often mistaken for settlement cracks, shrinkage cracks usually occur in the middle third of the wall and the footer beneath them remains intact. Shrinkage cracking is rarely serious, and in an older building may have been repaired previously. If the wall is unsound, its structural integrity sometimes can be restored by pressure-injecting concrete epoxy grout into the cracks or by adding pilasters.

- Sweeping or horizontal cracking of the foundation walls can be a major concern. The sweeping or horizontal cracking of brick or concrete block foundation walls may be caused by improper backfilling, vibration from the movement of heavy equipment or vehicles close to the wall, or by the swelling or freezing and heaving of water-saturated soils adjacent to the wall. Like drying shrinkage, sweeping or horizontal cracking may have occurred during the original construction and been compensated for at that time. Such distress, however, is potentially serious, as it indicates that the vertical supporting member (the foundation wall) that is carrying a portion of the structure above is bent or broken. It may be possible to push the wall back into place by careful hydraulic jacking and then reinforcing it with the addition of interior buttresses, or by pressure-injecting concrete epoxy grout into the wall. If outside ground conditions allow, the wall can be relieved of some lateral pressure by lowering the ground level around the building.

Soil. When expansive soils are suspected as the cause of the cracking, examine the exterior for sources of water, such as broken leaders or poor surface drainage. Frost heaving may be suspected if the damage is above the local frost depth or if it occurred during an especially cold period.

Non-Expansive Soils

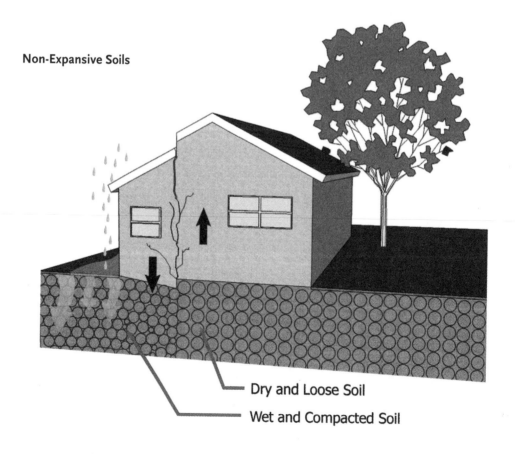

Dry and Loose Soil

Wet and Compacted Soil

6.5 Above-Ground Masonry Walls

For above-ground masonry walls, look for:

Brick wall cracking associated with thermal and moisture movement. Above-ground brick walls expand in warm weather (particularly if facing south or west) and contract in cool weather. This builds up stresses in the walls that may cause a variety of cracking patterns, depending on the configuration of the wall and the number and location of openings. Such cracks are normally cyclical and will open and close with the seasons. They will grow wider in cold weather and narrower in hot weather. Look for cracking at the corners of long walls, walls with abrupt changes in cross-section (such as at a row of windows), walls with abrupt turns or jogs, and in transitions from one- to two-story walls. These are the weak points that have the least capacity for stress.

Common moisture and thermal movement cracking includes:

- horizontal or diagonal cracks near the ground at piers in long walls due to horizontal shearing stresses between the upper wall and the wall where it enters the ground. The upper wall can thermally expand but its movement at ground level is moderated by earth temperatures. Such cracks extend across the piers from one opening to another along the line of least resistance. This condition is normally found only in walls of substantial length;

- vertical cracks near the end walls due to thermal movement. A contracting wall does not have the tensile strength to pull its end walls with it as it moves inward, causing it or the end walls to crack vertically where they meet;

- vertical cracks in short offsets and setbacks caused by the thermal expansion of the longer walls that are adjacent to them. The shorter walls are bent by this thermal movement and crack vertically;

- vertical cracks near the top and ends of the façade due to the thermal movement of the wall. This may indicate poorly bonded masonry. Cracks will tend to follow openings upward; and

- cracks around stone sills and lintels caused by the expansion of the masonry against both ends of a tight-fitting stone piece that cannot be compressed.

Cracks associated with thermal and moisture movement are usually only cosmetic problems. After their cause has been determined, they should be repaired with a flexible sealant, since filling such cyclic cracks with mortar will simply cause the masonry to crack in another location. Cracks should be examined by a structural engineer.

Brick wall cracking can be associated with freeze-thaw cycles and corrosion. Brick walls often exhibit distress due to the expansion of freezing water or the rusting of embedded metals.

Look for cracking around sills, cornices, eaves, chimneys, parapets, and other elements subject to water penetration, which is usually due to the migration of water into the masonry. The water expands upon freezing, breaking the bond between the mortar and

Cracking

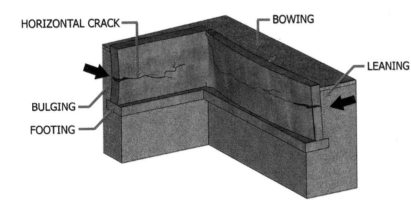

HORIZONTAL CRACK
BOWING
BULGING
FOOTING
LEANING

the masonry and eventually displacing the masonry itself. The path of the water through the wall is indicated by the pattern of deterioration.

Look for cracking around iron or steel lintels, which is caused by the expansive force of corrosion that builds up on the surface of the metal. This exerts great pressure on the surrounding masonry and displaces it, since corroded iron can expand to many times its original thickness. Structural iron and steel concealed within the masonry, if exposed to moisture, can also corrode and cause cracking and displacement of its masonry cover. Rust stains usually indicate that corrosion is the cause of the problem. Check to make sure the joint between the masonry and the steel lintel that supports the masonry over an opening is clear and open. If the joint has been sealed, the sealant or mortar should be removed.

These conditions can usually can be corrected by repairing or replacing corroded metal components and by repairing and re-pointing the masonry. Where cracking is severe, portions of the wall may have to be reconstructed. Cracks should be further examined by a structural engineer.

Look for wall cracking or displacement associated with the structural failure of building elements. Structure-related problems, aside from those caused by differential settlement or earthquakes, are usually found over openings and less commonly under roof eaves or in areas of structural overloading.

Such problems include:

- cracking or displacement of masonry over openings, resulting from the deflection or failure of the lintels or arches that span the openings. In older masonry walls with wood lintels, cracking will occur as the wood sags or decays. Iron and steel lintels also cause cracking as they deflect over time. Concrete and stone lintels occasionally bow and sometimes crack.

  Masonry arches of brick or stone may crack or fail when there is wall movement or when their mortar joints deteriorate.

When such lintel deflections or arch failures occur, the masonry above may be supporting itself and will exhibit step cracks, beginning at the edges of the opening and joining in an inverted V above the opening's midpoint. Correcting such problems usually means replacing failed components and rebuilding the area above the opening.

- cracking or outward displacement under the eaves of a pitched roof due to failure in the horizontal roof ties that results in the roof spreading outward. The lateral thrust of the roof on the masonry wall may cause it to crack horizontally just below the eaves or to move outward with the roof. The roof will probably be leaking, as well. When this occurs, examine the roof structure carefully to ascertain whether there is a tying failure. If so, additional horizontal ties or tension members will have to be added and, if possible, the roof pulled back into place. The damaged masonry can then be repaired. The weight can also be transferred to interior walls. Jacking of the ridge and rafters is possible, too.

Masonry walls sometimes show signs of bulging as they age. A wall itself may bulge, or the bulge may only be in the outer withe. Bulging often takes place so slowly that the masonry doesn't crack, and, therefore, it may go unnoticed over a long period of time. The bulging of the whole wall is usually due to thermal or moisture expansion of the wall's outer surface or to contraction of the inner withe. This expansion is not completely reversible because once the wall and its associated structural components are pushed out of place, they can rarely be completely pulled back to their original positions.

The effects of the cyclical expansion of a wall are cumulative, and after many years, the wall will show a detectable bulge. Inside the building, separation cracks may occur on the inside face of the wall at floors, walls and ceilings. Bulging of only the outer masonry withe is usually due to the same gradual process of thermal or moisture expansion: masonry debris accumulates behind the bulge and prevents the course from returning to its original position. In very old buildings, small wall bulges may result from the decay and collapse of an internal wood lintel or wood-bonding course, which can cause the inner course to settle and the outer course to bulge outward.

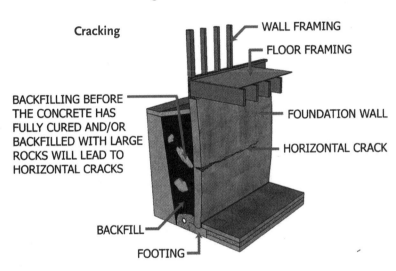

Cracking

WALL FRAMING

FLOOR FRAMING

BACKFILLING BEFORE THE CONCRETE HAS FULLY CURED AND/OR BACKFILLED WITH LARGE ROCKS WILL LEAD TO HORIZONTAL CRACKS

FOUNDATION WALL

HORIZONTAL CRACK

BACKFILL

FOOTING

Bulging of walls. When wall bulges occur in solid masonry walls, the walls may be insufficiently tied to the structure or their mortar may have lost its bond strength. Large bulges must be tied back to the structure; the star-shaped anchors on the exterior of masonry walls of many older buildings are examples of such ties (check with local building ordinances on their use). Small bulges in the outer masonry course often can be pinned to the inner course or dismantled and rebuilt.

Leaning of walls. Masonry walls that lean represent a serious and uncommon condition that is usually caused by poor design and construction practices, particularly inadequate structural tying or poor foundation work.

Brick veneer walls. Brick veneer walls are subject to the forces of differential settlement, moisture- and thermal-related cracking, and the effects of freezing and corrosion.

Look for:

- cracks caused by frame shrinkage, which are most likely to be found around fixed openings where the independent movement of the veneer wall is restrained;

- bulging, which is caused by inadequate or deteriorated ties between the brick and the wall that it is held upon; and

- vertical cracking at corners or horizontal cracking near the ground caused by thermal movement of the wall, which is similar to that in solid masonry or masonry cavity walls, but possibly more pronounced in well-insulated buildings because of the reduction in the moderating effect from interior temperatures. Thermal cracks are cyclic and should be filled with a flexible sealant. Where there is severe cracking, expansion joints may have to be installed.

Problems associated with parapet walls. Parapet walls often exhibit signs of distress and deterioration due to their full exposure to the weather, the splashing of water from the roof, differential movement, the lack of restraint by vertical loads or horizontal bracing, and the lack of adequate expansion joints.

At parapets:

- horizontal cracking at the roof line due to differential thermal movement between the roof line and the wall below, which is exposed to moderating interior temperatures. The parapet may eventually lose all bond except that due to friction and its own weight, and may be pushed out by ice formation on the roof;

- bowing due to thermal and moisture expansion when the parapet is restrained from lengthwise expansion by end walls or adjacent buildings. The wall will usually bow outward because that is the direction of least resistance;

- overhanging the end walls when the parapet is not restrained on its ends. The problem is often the most severe when one end is restrained and the other is not;

- random vertical cracking near the center of the wall due to thermal contraction;

- deterioration of parapet masonry due to excessive water penetration through inadequate coping or flashing, if any, which, when followed by freeze-thaw cycles, causes masonry spalling and mortar deterioration; and

- fire damage to brick masonry walls. Masonry walls exposed to fire will resist damage in proportion to their thickness. Examine the texture and color of the masonry units and probe their mortar. If they are intact and their basic color is unchanged, they can be considered serviceable. If they undergo a color change, consult a qualified structural engineer. Hollow masonry units should be examined for internal cracking by cutting into the wall, where possible. Such units may need replacement if seriously damaged.

6.6 Chimneys

If you have a chimney, look at it. Chimneys have greater exposure to the weather than most building elements and have no lateral support from the point where they emerge from the roof. Problems can develop at any point in time as the house ages.

What to look for:

An inadequate foundation can cause differential settlement of the chimney, but the foundation is underground and not readily visible. If the chimney is part of an exterior wall, it will tend to lean away from the wall and crack where it is joined to other masonry. In some cases, the chimney can be tied to the building.

A chimney sweep can monitor the chimney structure for you. Masonry at the top of the chimney stack can deteriorate due to a deteriorated cap that allows water into the masonry below and exposes it to freeze-thaw cycles. This cap is often made of a tapered layer of mortar, called a cement wash, which cracks and breaks after several years. If the cap is mortar and the chimney has a hood, repair the mortar. If the cap is mortar and the chimney does not have a hood, replace the mortar with a stone or concrete cap. If the cap is stone or concrete, repair it or replace it.

The chimney could lean where it projects above the roof due to deteriorated mortar joints caused either by wind-induced swaying of the chimney, or by sulfate attack from flue gases and particulates within the chimney if the chimney is not protected by a tight flue liner. Deteriorated mortar joints should be re-pointed, and unstable chimneys or those with a noticeable lean should be dismantled and rebuilt.

6.7 Wood Structural Components

Wood structural components in small residential buildings are often directly observable only in attics, crawlspaces or basements. Elsewhere, they are concealed by floor, wall and ceiling materials. Common signs of wood structural problems include sloping or springy floors, wall and ceiling cracks, wall bulges, and sticking doors and windows, although many of these problems can be attributable to differential settlement of the foundation or problems with exterior masonry bearing walls.

The five types of problems commonly associated with such components in small residential buildings include: deflection and warping; fungal and insect attack; fire; connection failure; and improper alteration.

When failures in wood structural components occur, they usually involve individual wood members and rarely result in the failure of the entire structure. Instead, an elastic adjustment takes place that redistributes stresses to other components in the building.

Deflection, warping, and associated problems. Some deflection of wood structural components and assemblies is common in older buildings and normally can be tolerated. Once permanently deflected, a wood structural component cannot be straightened.

Warping of individual wood components almost always takes place early in the life of a building. It will usually cause only superficial damage.

With wood, look for:

- **floor sagging** near stairway openings due to gradual deflection of the unsupported floor framing. This is a common problem in older houses and usually does not present a structural problem;

- **floor sagging** beneath door jambs resulting from improper support below the jamb. This can be a structural concern. If needed, additional bracing can be added between the joists where the sag occurs;

Inspecting Beams for Sag

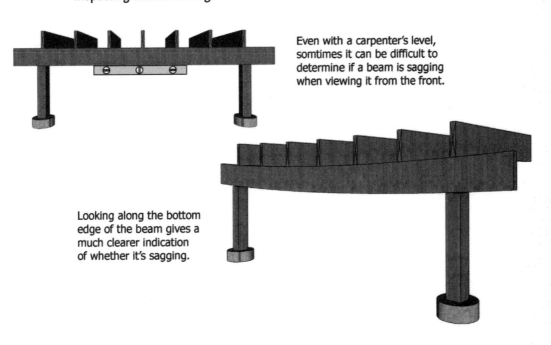

Even with a carpenter's level, somtimes it can be difficult to determine if a beam is sagging when viewing it from the front.

Looking along the bottom edge of the beam gives a much clearer indication of whether it's sagging.

- **loss of bearing** in beams and joists over foundation walls, piers or columns due to movement caused by long-term deflection of the wood beams or joists, differential movement of the foundation elements, localized crushing, or wood decay. Monitor the bearing and connections of all exposed structural elements that are in contact with the foundation, and look for symptoms of bearing failure where these elements are concealed, such as bowing or sloping in the floor above, and cracking or tilting of foundation walls, piers and columns;

- **sagging, sloping or springing** floors due to foundation settlement, excessive spans, cut or drilled structural elements, overloading, or removal of supporting walls or columns on the floor above or below. In older buildings, columns or walls that helped support or stabilize the floor above may have been removed during a previous alteration; conversely, partitions, bathroom or kitchen renovations, or similar remodeling may have been placed on a floor not designed to support such additional loads. Depending on the circumstances, sagging, sloping or springing floors may be anything from an annoyance to an indication of a potentially serious structural problem. Check below the floor for adequate supports and bearing and for sound connections between structural elements. Look for signs of supporting walls that have been removed, missing joist hangers, and for inappropriate cuts or holes in joists for plumbing, electrical, or HVAC lines or ducts. Also, look for signs of insect or fungal attack;

- **cracking in interior walls** around openings, which may be caused by inadequate, deflected or warped framing around the openings, differential settlement of the interior of masonry load-bearing walls, or problems in the exterior masonry wall. Cracking due to framing problems is usually not serious, although it may be a cosmetic concern that can be corrected only by breaking into the wall;

- **sagging in sloped roofs** resulting from too many layers of roofing material, failure of fire-retardant plywood roof sheathing, inadequate bracing, or undersized rafters. Sometimes, three or more layers of shingles are applied to a roof, greatly increasing its dead load. Or, when an attic story has been made into a habitable space or otherwise altered, collar beams or knee walls may have been removed. A number of factors, such as increases in snow and wind loads, poor structural design, and construction errors result in undersized rafters. Look for all these conditions;

- **failure of fire-retardant plywood (FRP)** used at party walls between dwelling units in some townhouses, row houses and multiple dwellings, which is not uncommon. Premature failure of the material could be due to excessive heat in the attic space. On the exterior, sagging of the roof adjacent to a party wall often is apparent. On the interior, check for darkening of the plywood surface, similar to charring, as an indication of failure that requires replacement of the FRP with a product of comparable fire resistance and structural strength;

- **spreading of the roof downward and outward** due to inadequate tying. Look for missing collar beams, inadequate tying of rafters and ceiling joists at the eaves, or inadequate tying of ceiling joists that act as tension members from one side of the roof to the other. Altered trusses can also cause this problem. Check trusses for cut, failed or removed members, and for fasteners that have failed, been completely removed or partially disconnected. Spreading can be halted by adequate bracing or tying, but there may be damage to masonry walls below the eaves. It is possible that the roof can be jacked back to its proper position;

- **deflection of flat roofs** due to too great a span, overloading, or improper support of joists beneath the roof. This is a common problem and is usually of no great concern unless it results in leaking and subsequent damage to the structure, or unless it causes water to pond on the roof, thereby creating unacceptable dead loads. In both cases, the roof will have to be strengthened or leveled; and

- **fungal and insect attack.** The moisture content of properly protected wood structural components in buildings usually does not exceed 10 to 15%, which is well below the 25 to 30% required to promote decay by the fungi that cause rot or to promote attack by many of the insects that feed on or inhabit wood. Dry wood will never decay. Check all structural and non-structural wood components for signs of fungus and insect infestation, including wood stains, fungi, termite shelter tubes, entry and exit holes, signs of tunneling, soft or discolored wood, small piles of sawdust or frass, and related signs of infestation.

You can probe all suspect wood with a sharp instrument. Building inspectors check moisture content with moisture measurement devices. Wood with a meter reading of more than 20 to 25% should be thoroughly examined for rot and infestation. Sound wood will separate in long fibrous splinters, but decayed wood will lift up in short irregular pieces.

Check these exterior components:

- shelter tubes, which can be found at foundation walls, in the cracks and corners;

- where wood is in contact with the ground, such as wood pilings, porch and deck supports, porch lattices, wood steps, adjacent fences and nearby wood piles;

- frames and sills around basement or lower-level window and door frames, and the base of frames around garage doors;

- wood framing adjacent to slab-on-grade porches or patios; and

- wood near or in contact with roofs, drains, window wells or other areas exposed to periodic wetting from rain or lawn sprinklers, etc.

Check these interior components:

- wood-frame basement partitions;

- spaces around or within interior foundation walls and floors, crawlspaces, piers, columns or pipes that might harbor shelter tubes, including cavities and cracks;

- the sill plate that covers the foundation wall, and joists, beams, and other wood components in contact with them;

The Pick Test

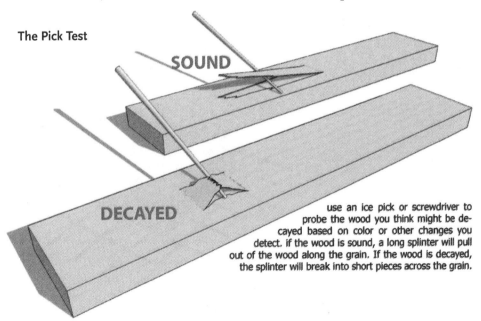

SOUND

DECAYED

use an ice pick or screwdriver to probe the wood you think might be decayed based on color or other changes you detect. if the wood is sound, a long splinter will pull out of the wood along the grain. If the wood is decayed, the splinter will break into short pieces across the grain.

- baseboard trim in slab-on-grade foundation;

- subflooring and joists below the kitchen, bathroom and laundry area; and

- roof sheathing and framing in the attic around chimneys, vents and other openings.

6.8 Iron and Steel Structural Components

Metal structural components used in homes are usually limited to beams and pipe columns in basements, angles over small masonry openings, and beams over long spans. These components are almost always made of steel.

Problems with iron and steel structural components usually involve corrosion. Monitoring is needed.

Steel Angle Lintels

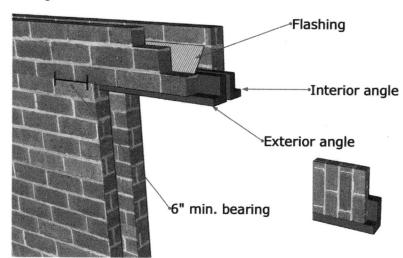

Lintels and other embedded metal components in exterior masonry walls can corrode and, in time, become severely weakened themselves. Rain and snow often contain carbonic, sulfuric, nitric or hydrochloric acid that lowers the pH of rainwater, thereby accelerating corrosion. Check the areas of embedded iron and steel. Corrosion can also displace surrounding masonry by popping off mortar joints at brick walls.

Columns should be checked for adequate connections at their base and top, and for corrosion at their base if they rest at ground level.

6.9 Concrete Structural Components

Concrete is commonly used for grade and below-grade level floors and for footings. Concrete also may be used for foundations, beams, floors above grade, porches or patios built on grade, exterior stairs and stoops, sills, and occasionally as a precast or poured-in-place lintel or beam over masonry openings. Concrete structural components are reinforced. Welded-steel wire mesh is used in floors at and below grade, patios built on grade, walks and drives, and short-span, light-load lintels. All other concrete structural components are usually reinforced with steel bars.

Welded Wire Fabric

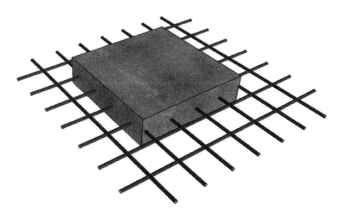

Look for cracking at:

- corners and openings in concrete foundations below masonry exterior walls due to drying shrinkage of concrete walls. This cracking will occur early in the life of the building. Minor cracks can be filled with mortar and major cracks with concrete epoxy; and

- interior slabs on grade, usually due to shrinkage or minor settlement below the slab. If cracking is near and parallel to foundation walls, it may have been caused by the movement of the walls or footers. Cracking can also result from soil swelling (expanding) beneath the slab, a condition that may be caused by water from clogged or broken basement or footer drains. Cracking of exterior concrete elements, such as porches, patios and stairs, is usually due to heaving from frost or nearby tree roots, freeze-thaw cycles, or settlement.

According to the Standards of Practice:

The inspector should inspect the basement, foundation, crawlspace, and visible structural components. The inspector should report any general indications of foundation movement that he/she observes, such as, but not limited to: sheetrock cracks, brick cracks, out-of-square door frames, and floor slopes.

Inspectors do not perform engineering or architectural services. They do not report upon the adequacy of any structural system or component.

Chapter 7: Plumbing System

7.1 Water Service Entry

Curb valve. A homeowner should know where the curb valve is located. It is the way for the main water supply to be turned off. It is typically located at the junction of the public water main and the house service main, usually at the street. The curb valve is typically the responsibility of the municipal water department.

House service main. The house service main begins at the curb valve and ends at the inside wall of the building at the master shutoff valve.

Main (or master) water shutoff valve. A master shutoff valve should be located where the house service main enters the building. If the water meter is not located inside the building, it will likely be outside in an underground crock. Home inspectors typically do not test this main valve during a visual-only inspection.

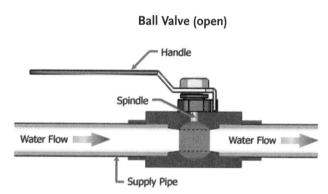

Ball Valve (open)

Handle

Spindle

Water Flow

Water Flow

Supply Pipe

Water meter. The water meter is normally the property of the municipal water company and may be located near the street, adjacent to the house, or within the house. If the water meter is located inside the house, look for two shutoff valves: one on the street-side and one on the house-side of the meter.

7.2 Interior Water Distribution

All piping, regardless of composition, should be monitored for wet spots, discoloration, pitting, mineral deposits, and leaking or deteriorated fittings.

Distribution piping. Distribution piping consists of supply mains and fixture risers. Most supply pipes can be seen from the basement or from the crawlspace, but the riser pipes are usually concealed within walls and cannot be readily examined.

The two most important factors in understanding distribution piping are the material and age.

Galvanized steel piping is subject to rusting and accumulates more mineral deposits than other piping materials. Rusted fittings and rust-colored water, particularly from hot water lines, are signs of advanced deterioration. Low rates of flow and low water pressure are likely

to be caused by galvanized steel piping clogged with rust and mineral deposits. If galvanized steel piping is found, consider replacing it.

Brass piping is of two varieties: yellow and red. Red is more common and has the longer service life—up to 70 years or more. The service life of yellow brass is about 40 years. Old brass piping is subject to pinhole leaking due to pitting caused by the chemical removal of its zinc content by minerals in the water. Often, water leaking from the pinhole openings will evaporate before dripping and leave whitish mineral deposits. Whitish deposits may also form around threaded joints, usually the most vulnerable part of a brass piping system. Brass piping with such signs of deterioration should be replaced.

Copper piping came into widespread use in most parts of the country in the 1930s and has a normal service life of 50 years or more. Copper lines and joints are highly durable and usually not subject to clogging by mineral deposits. Leakage usually occurs near joints.

Copper Supply Pipes

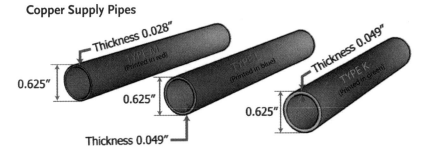

Plastic piping (ABS, PE, PB, PVC, CPVC and PEX) is a relatively new plumbing material and, if properly installed, supported, and protected from sunlight and mechanical damage, should last indefinitely. However, polybutylene (PB) pipe and fittings have been found to be unreliable for plumbing applications, resulting in several class-action lawsuits. Funds resulting from these suits are controlled by local jurisdictions. Check with local authorities or consumer advocate groups for details if your home has this type of piping.

Some newer buildings use a manifold off the water main to distribute cold water and a manifold off the water heater to distribute hot water. From the manifold, flexible plastic pipes are snaked through floors and walls to each plumbing fixture.

Lead piping used for water supply and distribution may be found in very old structures and may pose a health hazard to building occupants.

7.3 Drain, Waste and Vent Piping

Fixture traps. Fixture traps are designed to hold a water seal that blocks the entry of sewer gases into the house's interior through the fixture drain. Watch for clogs and water leaks at water traps.

Vents. Vents equalize the atmospheric pressure within the waste drainage system to prevent siphoning of the water seals in the building's fixture traps. Vents should be unobstructed and open above the roof.

Drain lines. Drain lines direct wastewater from the fixture trap through the building to the sewer or septic system. Monitor for water drips and leaks located at loose cleanout fittings.

7.4 Tank Water Heater

A tank water heater consists of a glass-lined or vitreous, enamel-coated steel tank covered by an insulated metal jacket. It is gas-fired, oil-fired or electrically heated.

- Gas-fired tank water heaters have an average life expectancy of about six to 12 years. They have a fairly high recovery rate.

- Oil-fired heaters have an average life similar to that of gas-fired heaters. Their recovery rate is also high.

- Electric water heaters have an estimated service life of five to 10 years. They have a low recovery rate and thus require a larger storage tank.

Plan to replace a tank that is near the end of its life expectancy.

Watch for signs of leakage on the bottom of the tank, such as rust or water stains at fuel-burning components or on the floor. Leaking tanks cannot usually be repaired and, therefore, must be replaced entirely.

As part of a maintenance plan, the tank should be drained regularly to remove sediment and rust.

Check the temperature/pressure relief-valve (sometimes found on the top or on the side of the tank), and for a discharge pipe that extends from the valve to a few inches from the floor, a floor drain, or the building exterior, depending on local code requirements. This pipe should never be dripping or leaking water.

Monitor for soot or carbon deposits. Any soot or carbon that has accumulated below the draft hood of a water heater may indicate a restricted flue or chimney, or, more commonly, back-drafting caused by insufficient make-up air.

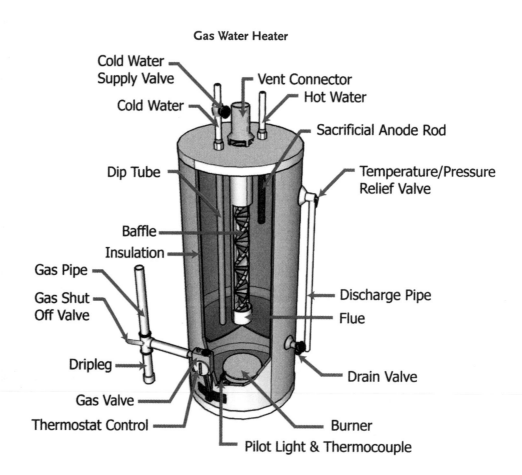

Gas Water Heater

7.5 Domestic Coil Water Heater (with Boiler)

Tankless domestic coil water heaters consist of small-diameter pipes coiled inside of or in a separate casing adjacent to a hot water boiler. They are designed for a rate of water flow of usually 3 to 4 gallons per minute. The recovery rate of a domestic coil water heater is instantaneous for low demand and will vary for high demand. The life expectancy of a domestic coil water heater is limited only by the deterioration of its coils and by the service life of the boiler to which it is attached.

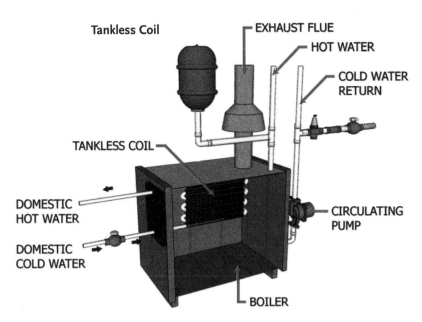

Tankless Coil

EXHAUST FLUE
HOT WATER
COLD WATER RETURN

TANKLESS COIL

DOMESTIC HOT WATER

DOMESTIC COLD WATER

CIRCULATING PUMP

BOILER

Monitor a tankless coil water heater by checking its performance (or ability to produce hot water on demand) and by checking the area where the coil is attached to the boiler. Over time, water may start to leak from the gasket area or the bolts at the front mounting plate where the tankless coil is located at the boiler.

Monitor the plumbing connections and joints around the heater mounting plate for rust, water stains and mineral deposits.

7.6 Private Well

Location and water quality. A homeowner should know the location of their private well. Ideally, a well that supplies drinking water is located uphill from the building and from any storm or sanitary sewer system piping. Standards usually require that the well be a minimum of 50 feet from a septic tank and 100 feet from any part of the absorption field. Local codes may have different separation distances based on the percolation rates of the local soils.

Pumps. Two kinds of deep-well pumps are in common use: the jet pump and the submersible pump.

A jet pump is mounted above the well casing, and two pipes should extend into it; if there is only one pipe leading into the casing, the well is less than 25 feet deep and may have inherent performance problems. Submersible pumps are located at the bottom of the well casing (submerged), and a single discharge pipe and an electrical supply cable extend

from the top of the casing. The life expectancy of deep-well pumps is 10 years or longer, depending on the type. Submersible pumps are usually the most long-lasting and trouble-free.

Two-Line Jet Pump

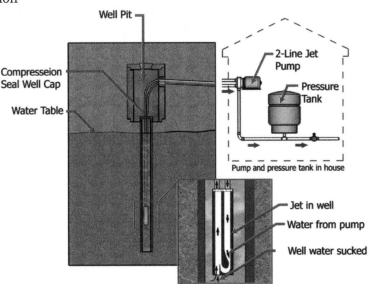

Well Pit

Compresseion Seal Well Cap

Water Table

2-Line Jet Pump

Pressure Tank

Pump and pressure tank in house

Jet in well

Water from pump

Well water sucked

Pressure tank. A tank under low air pressure (a hydropneumatic tank) should be located in either the well house or the building's basement. This tank regulates water pressure and flow.

Water tests. Consult your home inspector about sampling the water quality and inspecting the well system every year. Water should be analyzed for the presence of bacterial contamination and for its mineral content.

7.7 Septic System

Location and layout. The homeowner should know the layout of the existing septic system. The absorption field should not be disturbed by new construction or vehicular traffic, or covered by fill, trees or dense vegetation. No stormwater should be directed into the septic system. A typical system has an average life expectancy of 15 to 20 years under normal conditions.

Septic tank. If properly maintained, it should be pumped every two to three years. Keep records about pumping. Lack of periodic pumping will cause solids to be carried into the absorption field, clogging the leaching beds and shortening their useful life.

Signs of a clogged absorption field are the presence of dark green vegetation over the leaching beds throughout the growing season (caused by nutrient-laden wastes being pushed up through the soil), wet or soggy areas in the field, or distinct sewage odors.

Septic Tank

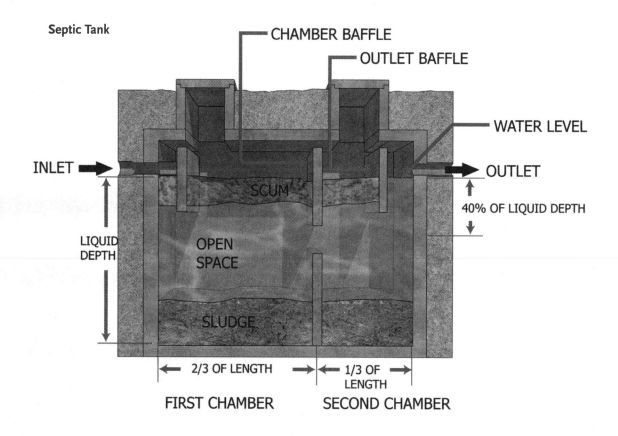

7.8 Gas Supply in Seismic Regions

Service entrance. If the building is in seismic zones 3 or 4 (California and portions of Alaska, Arkansas, Hawaii, Idaho, Missouri, Montana, Nevada, Oregon, Utah, Wyoming and Washington), the gas service should not be vulnerable to differential movement where the piping enters the building. Look for adequate clearance or for flexible connections.

Emergency shutoff. If the building is in seismic zone 4 (portions of Alaska and California, and small parts of Idaho, Montana and Wyoming), look for an automatic emergency shutoff valve for the entire house.

According to the Standards of Practice:

The inspector should inspect and describe the water supply, drain, waste and main fuel shutoff valves, water main valve and shutoff valve. The inspector is not required to determine the size, temperature, age or life expectancy of the water heater source. Home inspectors are not septic system inspectors.

Chapter 8: Electrical System

The primary components are the service entry, service panel, and branch circuits. In unaltered buildings built since about 1940, the electrical system is likely to be intact and safe, although it may not provide the capacity required for the use of the home. Electrical capacity can be easily increased by bringing additional capacity in from the street and adding a larger service panel between the service entry and the existing panel. Existing circuits can continue to use the existing panel and new circuits can be fed through the new panel.

The electrical systems of residential buildings built prior to about 1940 may require overhaul or replacement, depending on the condition of the electrical system. Parts of these older systems may function adequately.

8.1 Service Entry

Service. "Service" is a term used to describe the conductors and equipment for delivering electricity from the utility company to the wiring system of the building served. Only one is typically installed for a dwelling. A minimum of 100-amp service is needed for a single residence.

Service panel. It is typically referred to as the panelboard or main electrical panel. The first point of disconnect for the conductors from the utility company is at the main panel.

Overhead wires. Overhead wires from the street should be higher than 10 feet above the ground, not in contact with tree branches or other obstacles, and not reachable from nearby windows or other accessible areas. The wires should be securely attached to the building and have drip loops where they enter the weatherhead. Wires should not be located over swimming pools.

Electric meter. The electric meter and its base should be weatherproof and securely fastened. Advise the utility company of any problems with the meter.

Service entrance conductor. The insulation of the service entrance conductor should be completely intact. If the main service panel is located inside the building, the conductor's passage through the wall should be sealed against moisture.

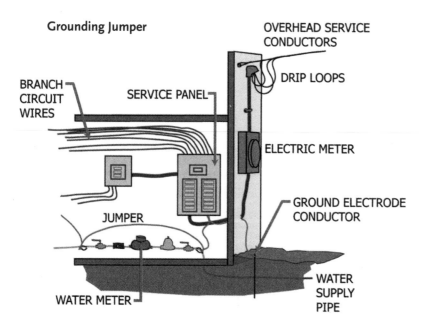

Grounding Jumper

OVERHEAD SERVICE CONDUCTORS

DRIP LOOPS

BRANCH CIRCUIT WIRES

SERVICE PANEL

ELECTRIC METER

JUMPER

GROUND ELECTRODE CONDUCTOR

WATER METER

WATER SUPPLY PIPE

8.2 Main Electrical Service Panel (Breaker Box)

The main electrical service panel is the distribution center for electrical service within the building. The primary function of the breakers or fuses (over-current protection devices) is to protect the house wiring from overloads.

All service panels must have covers or dead fronts. All openings should be closed.

Main disconnect. A means of disconnect for the service must be located either outside or inside the dwelling unit near the closest point of entrance of the service conductors. No more than six hand movements or no more than six circuit breakers may be used to disconnect all service. Typically, a main disconnect switch is required by the local authority. The main disconnect should be clearly marked to identify it as the service disconnect.

Condition and location. Water marks or rust on a service panel mounted inside the building may indicate water infiltration along the path of the service entrance conductor. Service panels mounted outdoors should be watertight. The service panel should have a workable space in front of it. The service panel should not be located inside a bathroom, over stairs, or inside a clothes closet.

Amperage rating. The amperage rating of the main disconnect should not be less than 60 amps. It should be labeled or identified as 100 amps or greater.

The ampacity of the service entrance conductor may be determined by a building inspector by noting the markings (if any) on the conductor cable and finding the rating. If the service entrance conductor is in a conduit, there may be markings on the conductor wires as they emerge from the conduit into the service panel. The ampere rating may be found on the service panel or service disconnect switch.

Grounding. A building inspector may be able to confirm that the service panel appears to be grounded. Its grounding conductor should run to an exterior grounding electrode, or be clamped to the metal water service inlet pipe between the exterior wall and the water meter.

The grounding electrode is a device that makes an electrical connection to the earth. A grounding electrode can be rebar in a footer, or a metal underground water supply pipe within 10 feet of contact with the earth, or a grounding rod.

Grounding Rod

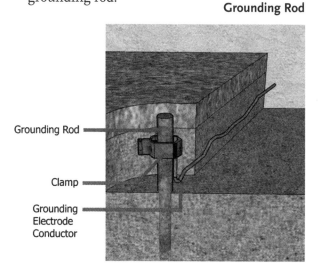

Grounding Rod

Clamp

Grounding Electrode Conductor

GFCI (ground-fault circuit interrupter). A GFCI is a device that adds a greater level of safety by reducing the risk of electric shock. Most building codes now require that GFCI protection be provided in wet locations, such as: all kitchen counter receptacles; all bathroom receptacles; all exterior receptacles; receptacles in laundry and utility rooms; receptacles next to wet bar sinks; all garage and unfinished basement receptacles, except receptacles that are not readily accessible or single receptacles for appliances that are not easily moved; receptacles near a pool, spa, or hot tub; and light fixtures near water.

Downstream. A GFCI may be wired in a branch circuit, which means other outlets and electrical devices may share the same circuit and breaker. When a properly wired GFCI trips, the other devices downstream from it will also lose power.

Ground-Fault Receptacle Protecting Entire Branch Circuit

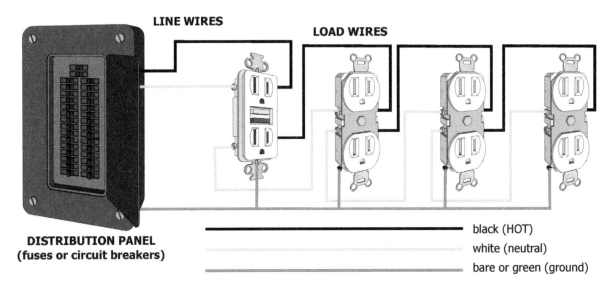

LINE WIRES

LOAD WIRES

DISTRIBUTION PANEL
(fuses or circuit breakers)

—— black (HOT)
—— white (neutral)
—— bare or green (ground)

If you have an outlet that doesn't work, and the breaker is not tripped, look for a GFCI outlet that may have tripped. The non-working outlet may be downstream from a GFCI device. The "dead" outlets may not be located near the GFCI outlet; they may be several rooms away or even on a different floor.

GFCI outlets should be tested periodically, at least once a year. All GFCI devices have test buttons.

AFCI (arc-fault circuit interrupter). All 15-amp and 20-amp, 120-volt circuits for dining rooms, living rooms, bedrooms, sunrooms, closets, hallways and similar areas must be AFCI-protected. An arc-fault circuit interrupter is a circuit breaker designed to prevent fires by detecting non-working electrical arcs and disconnecting power before the arc starts a fire. The AFCI distinguishes between a working arc that may occur in the brushes of a vacuum sweeper, light switch, or other household devices and a non-working arc that can occur in a lamp cord that has a broken conductor in the cord from overuse, for instance. Arc faults in a home are one of the leading causes of household fires.

AFCIs resemble GFCIs in that they both have test buttons, though it is important to distinguish between the two. GFCIs are designed to protect against electrical shock, while AFCIs are primarily designed to protect against fire.

Over-current protection. A breaker or fuse is referred to as an over-current protection device. It is recommended that the homeowner turn all circuit breakers on and off manually and make sure they are in functional condition.

The rating of the fuse or circuit breaker for each branch circuit may be checked by a building inspector or electrician. The amperage of the fuse or circuit breaker should not exceed the capacity of the wiring in the branch circuit it protects. Most household circuits use #14 copper wire, which should have 15-amp protection. There may be one or more circuits with #12 copper wire, which should have 20-amp protection. Large appliances, such as electric water heaters and central air conditioners, may require 30-amp service, which is normally supplied by #10 copper wire. An electric range requires a 40-amp or 50-amp service with #6 copper wire.

Identification. Each circuit should be clearly and specifically identified as to its purpose. No two circuits should be labeled the same. No circuit should be identified in a way that may be subject to change with occupancy. For example, no breaker should be labeled "Ben's room."

8.3 Branch Circuits

The oldest wiring system that may still be acceptable, and one still found fairly often in houses built before 1930, is knob-and-tube (K&T) wiring. This system utilizes porcelain insulators (knobs) for running wires through unobstructed spaces, and porcelain tubes for running wires through building components, such as studs and joists. Knob-and-tube wiring should be replaced during rehabilitation, but if it is properly installed, needs no modification, has adequate capacity, is properly grounded, has no failed insulation, and is otherwise in good condition, it can be an acceptable wiring system and is still allowed in many localities. Check with local building code officials. Also, check the terms and conditions of your homeowner's insurance policy to see if knob-and-tube wiring is excluded. The greatest problem with this type of wiring is its insulation, which turns dry and brittle with age and often falls off on contact, leaving the wire exposed. Knob-and-tube wiring is known to have caused house fires. Approved wire types include:

Conductor Markings

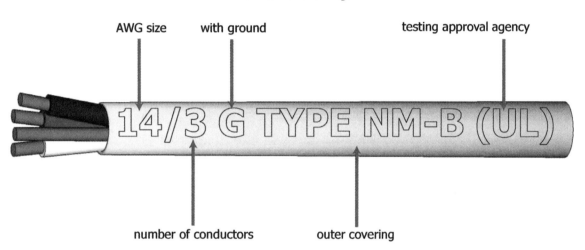

- NM (non-metallic) cable, often called by the trade name Romex®, a plastic covered-cable for use in dry locations (older NM cable may be cloth-covered);

- NMC, similar to NM but rated for damp locations;

- UF (underground feeder), a plastic-covered waterproof cable for use underground;

- AC (armored cable), also called BX, a flexible metal-covered cable;

- MC (metal-clad cable), a flexible metal-covered cable with a green insulated ground conductor; and

- EMT (electrical metallic tubing), also called "thinwall," a metal conduit through which the wires are run in areas where maximum protection is required.

Aluminum wire. Aluminum wire was installed in residential buildings primarily during the 1960s and early 1970s and is a potential fire hazard.

According to the U.S. Consumer Product Safety Commission, fires have been caused by the use of aluminum wiring in homes. Problems due to expansion and arcing at the connections can cause overheating between the wire and the devices, or at wire splices. The connections can become hot enough to start a fire.

Aluminum wire should be attached only to approved devices marked CO-ALR or CU-AL, or with connectors.

Problems with aluminum wiring occur at connections, so feel the cover plates for heat, smell for a distinctive odor in the vicinity of outlets and switches, and look for sparks and arcing in switches and outlets, and for flickering lights. Whenever possible, aluminum wire and its devices should be replaced with copper wire and devices appropriate for copper. It is difficult to find aluminum branch wiring in a home during a visual inspection. For a thorough investigation, an electrician should be hired.

Smoke detectors. After moving into a new home, consider replacing all of the smoke/fire detectors in the entire house. The building should have functioning smoke detectors. They should be wired to a power source and include a back-up battery. Smoke detectors do not last forever. Replace them according to the manufacturers' recommendations. Test the detectors regularly.

Replace batteries when you change your clocks for Daylight Saving Time changes.

According to the Standards of Practice:

The inspector is required to inspect the service panel and over-current devices, but is not required to operate or reset over-current devices. During a home inspection, a representative number of switches, receptacles, lighting fixtures, and AFCI-protected receptacles are inspected (but not each and every one).

The inspector should report the presence of solid-conductor aluminum branch circuit wiring only if it is readily visible. The measurement of the amperage or voltage of the electrical service is not required by the Standards. Exterior accent wiring is not part of a home inspection.

Chapter 9: HVAC System

Most HVAC (heating, ventilating and air-conditioning) systems in small residential buildings are relatively simple in design and operation. They consist of four components: controls, fuel supply, heating or cooling unit, and distribution system. The adequacy of heating and cooling is often quite subjective and depends upon occupant perceptions that are affected by the distribution of air, the location of return-air vents, air velocity, the sound of the system in operation, and similar characteristics.

9.1 Thermostatic Controls

Residential HVAC controls consist of one or more thermostats and a master shutoff switch for the heating or cooling unit.

Thermostats. Thermostats are temperature-sensitive switches that automatically control the heating or cooling system. Thermostats should be located in areas with average temperature conditions and away from heat sources, such as windows, water pipes and ducts.

Once a year, remove the thermostat cover and check for dust on the spring coil and dirty or corroded electrical contact points. Plan to replace worn or defective thermostats. There may be more than one thermostat. Sometimes, two thermostats separately control the heating and cooling system, and sometimes the living unit is divided into zones, each with its own thermostat.

Master (or service) shutoff switch. Every gas-burning and oil-burning system should have a master switch that serves as an emergency shutoff for the burner. Master shutoff switches are usually located near the burner unit or, if there is a basement, near the top of the stairs.

9.2 Fuel-Burning Unit

Oil-fired and gas-fired furnaces and boilers provide heat to the majority of small residential buildings. Such fuel-burning units, whether they are part of a warm-air or a hot-water system, should be maintained and monitored regularly.

No fuel-burning unit should be located directly off sleeping areas or close to combustible materials.

Seismic vulnerability. If the building is in a seismic zone, the HVAC unit should be attached to the structure with seismic bracing.

Fuel supply. Gas supply lines should be made of black iron or steel pipe (some jurisdictions allow copper lines with brazed connections). Shutoff valves should be easily accessible. A gas shutoff valve should be next to the HVAC unit.

Oil tanks should be maintained in accordance with local regulations. All tanks must be vented to the outside and have an outside fill pipe. Buried tanks normally have a 550-, 1,000- or 1,500-gallon capacity; basement tanks are usually sized to a 275-gallon capacity.

An oil filter should be installed on the oil supply line that runs from the storage tank to the oil burner. The filter needs to be serviced every year.

Ventilation and access. Make sure the fuel-burning unit has adequate combustion air and is easily accessible for servicing with at least 3 feet clear on each side of the unit.

Condition. On hot-air furnaces, look for signs of rust on the furnace jacket from basement dampness or flooding, and, if an air-conditioning evaporator coil is located over the furnace, look for rust caused by condensate overflow. On hot water boilers, look for rust caused by dampness or by leaking water lines and fittings.

Flame. Once the unit has been activated, closely observe the combustion process. In oil-fired units, the flame should be clear and smoke-free, and have a slight orange-yellow color. The flame height should be uniform.

Gas-fired units should have a flame that is primarily bluish in color. Check gas burners for rust and clogged ports. Soot or carbon build-up on the burners could be a sign of inefficient combustion. In oil-fired units, look for soot below the draft regulator, on top of the unit's housing, and around the burner. The odor of smoke near the unit is another sign of poor combustion.

Have a service technician service and clean the system each year. Keep maintenance records up to date.

9.3 Forced-Air Heating

Warm-air heating systems are of two types: forced-air and gravity. Gravity systems are occasionally still found in older single-family houses, but most gravity systems have been replaced or converted to forced-air.

Most forced-air systems use natural gas or fuel oil as the heat source, but some systems use electric resistance heaters or heat pumps. The circulation blower and air-distribution ductwork for electric resistance heating systems (and heat pumps) are identical to those of gas-fired and oil-fired warm-air systems and should be regularly serviced and maintained.

House Air Flow

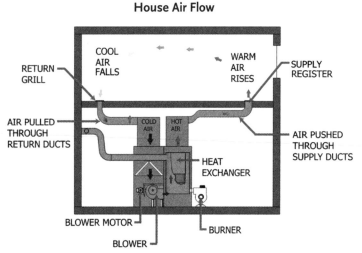

Heat exchanger. The heat exchanger is located downstream of the burner in gas-fired and oil-fired furnaces and separates the products of combustion from the air to be heated. It is critical that the heat exchanger be intact and contain no cracks or other openings that could allow combustion products into the warm-air distribution system. Visual detection of cracks, even by heating experts, is a difficult (if not impossible) process.

Monitor. Look for signs of soot at supply registers and smell for oil or gas vapors. Observe the burner flame as the furnace fan turns on; a disturbance or color change in the flame may indicate air leakage through a crack in the exchanger. A major cause of premature exchanger failure is water leakage from humidifiers or blocked air-conditioner condensate lines. Check for signs of water leakage. The durability of the heat exchanger determines the service life of the furnace.

Circulation blower fan. If the fan is worn or misaligned, or has excessive dust and dirt on the fins, the fan may rumble or make unusual sounds that may actually shake the ductwork.

Distribution system. The distribution system is made up of supply and return ducts, filters, dampers and registers. Supply and return ducts may be made of sheet metal, fiberglass or other materials. Check ducts for open joints and air leakage wherever the ducts are exposed. Air ducts can be cleaned by an HVAC contractor or a professional duct-cleaning contractor. Ducts could be cleaned every five years. Cleaning ducts is part of maintaining a healthy home. There should be no openings in return ducts in the same room as a combustion furnace.

Check the air filter. Air filters are usually located on the return-side of the furnace next to the blower, but they may be found anywhere in the distribution system. Check for their presence and examine their condition. The homeowner should check and replace the air filter every month (or according to the manufacturer's recommendations).

Humidifiers may be located in the supply air ducts. Ideally, they are not located in return air ducts because the moist air will pass through the heat exchanger and evaporator coil, rendering the humidification ineffective and corroding the heat exchanger. Humidifiers require regular maintenance.

Air Distribution System

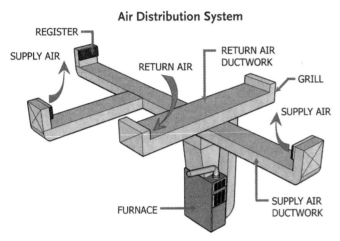

9.4 Forced Hot-Water or Hydronic System

Hot-water heating systems, like warm-air systems, include two types: forced or hydronic and gravity. Gravity systems are sometimes found in older single-family houses, but in most cases, such systems have been replaced or converted to a forced hot-water system. Gravity systems have no water pump and use larger piping. They tend to heat unevenly, are slow to respond, and can only heat spaces above the level of their boiler. Like gravity warm-air systems, they are considered inefficient. Forced hot-water systems are usually heated by gas-fired or oil-fired boilers.

Boilers

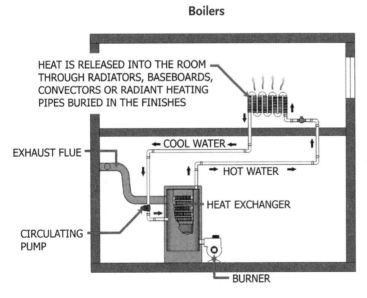

Boilers. Monitor all boilers for signs of corrosion and leakage. Most hot-water and steam-heating systems have steel boilers with a service life of about 20 years. Cast-iron boilers have a service life of about 30 years. Water leaking from the exchanger of the boiler is likely an indication of a major defect requiring replacement.

Expansion tank. The expansion tank is usually located above the boiler and is connected to the hot-water distribution piping. The pressure-relief valve should discharge water from the system when the boiler pressure reaches 30 psi.

Look for signs of water near the valve or below it on the floor. High-pressure conditions are usually due to a waterlogged expansion tank. If the boiler also generates domestic hot water, high pressure may be caused by cracks in the coils of the water heater, since the domestic water-supply pressure usually exceeds 30 psi. Any water drips coming from the relief valve are unacceptable and may indicate a safety hazard.

Circulating pump and controls. The circulating pump forces hot water through the system at a constant flow rate, usually stated in gallons per minute (gpm). It should be located adjacent to the boiler on the return pipe near the boiler. Monitor the condition and operation of the pump itself. Listen for smooth operation. A loud pump may have bad bearings or a faulty motor. Look at the gasket seal between the motor and the pump housing for signs of leakage. Look for scorching at all electrical wiring and connections. Circulating pumps should be lubricated regularly according to the owner's manual.

Distribution piping. The forced hot-water distribution system consists of distribution piping, radiators and control valves.

Distribution piping may be one of three types: series-loop; one-pipe; and two-pipe.

In a series-loop system, radiators are connected by one pipe in a series. In a one-pipe system, each radiator is separately attached to the water-distribution pipe with a regulating diverter fitting. A two-pipe system uses two pipes: one for supply water and one for return.

Monitor the distribution piping, valves, connections and radiators for water leaks.

Radiators and control valves. Radiators include three types: cast-iron (freestanding or hung from the ceiling or wall); convector (which may have a circulating fan); and baseboard. Older residential buildings usually have cast-iron radiators that are extremely durable. Baseboard radiators are considered the most desirable for residential use because they are the least conspicuous and distribute heat most evenly throughout the room. Monitor them for water leaks. When a leak is detected, have a service technician flush the piping to check for galvanic corrosion.

9.5 Steam-Heating System

Steam-heating systems are seldom installed in small residential buildings but are still common in many older ones. They are simple in design and operation but require a higher level of maintenance than modern residential heating systems. A homeowner should have plans to keep the system maintained continuously.

Steam boiler controls. Unlike hot-water boilers, steam boilers operate only at about 75% full of water and at much lower pressures, usually 2 to 5 psi. Steam boilers should be equipped with a water level gauge, a pressure gauge, a high-pressure limit switch, a low water cut-off, and a safety valve.

Look at the water-level gauge that indicates the level of the water in the steam boiler. The gauge should normally read about half full, though

the actual level of the water is not critical as long as the level is showing. If the gauge is full of water, the boiler is flooded and water must be drained from the system. If the gauge is empty, the boiler water level is too low and must be filled either manually through the fill valve or automatically through the automatic water-feed valve, if the boiler has one. An unsteady, up-and-down motion of water in the gauge could mean the boiler is clogged with sediment or is otherwise operating incorrectly and must be repaired. The clarity of the boiler water should be checked when checking the gauge. If the gauge is too dirty to judge the water level, it needs to be removed and cleaned. Consider hiring an HVAC professional to maintain the system.

Steam-distribution pipes. The steam-distribution system consists of distribution piping, radiators and control valves. Distribution piping may have either a one-pipe or two-pipe configuration.

In a one-pipe system, steam from the boiler rises under pressure through the pipes to the radiators. There, it displaces air by evacuation through the radiator vent valves, condenses on the radiator's inner surface, and gives up heat. Steam condensate flows by gravity back through the same pipes to the boiler for reheating. Therefore, the pipes must be pitched no less than 1 inch in 10 feet in the direction of the boiler to ensure that the condensate does not block the steam in any part of the system. All piping and radiators must be located above the boiler in a one-pipe system.

In a two-pipe steam system, steam flows to the radiators in one pipe and condensate returns in another. A steam trap on the condensate-return line releases air displaced by the incoming steam. If the condensate-return piping is located below the level of the boiler, it should be brought back up to the level of the boiler and vented to the supply piping in a Hartford loop. This prevents a leak in the condensate return from emptying the boiler.

Steam-distribution piping should be checked for leaks at all valves and connections. Make sure all piping is properly pitched to drain toward the boiler. A pounding noise called water hammer may occur when oncoming steam meets water trapped in the system by improperly pitched distribution piping or by shutoff valves that are not fully closed or fully open.

The valve to the steam radiator should not be turned on partway (it must be either completely on or completely off) or banging may occur. Variable air-vent valves properly balance the system and can turn down the heat, if needed.

9.6 Electric-Resistance Heater

Electric-resistance heating elements are commonly used in heat-pump systems, wall heaters, radiant wall and ceiling panels, and baseboard heaters. They are less frequently used as a heat source for central warm-air or hot-water systems. Such heating devices require some maintenance.

Electric-resistance heaters. Electric-resistance heaters are used in warm-air and hot-water systems and in heat pumps. They incorporate one or more heavy-duty heating elements that are actuated by sequence relays on demand from the thermostat.

Electric wall heaters. These compact devices are often used as supplementary heating units. They may have one or more electric heating elements, depending on their size. Wall heaters often have a small circulation fan. Look for dirt buildup on the fan blades and motor housing.

Radiant wall and ceiling panels. Electric heating panels that are embedded in wall or ceiling surfaces cannot be directly inspected, but all radiant surfaces should be monitored for signs of surface and structural damage.

Baseboard heaters. Baseboard heater heating fins can be damaged and become clogged with dust. Once a year, remove the heater covers and clean the unit. Bent heating fins can often be straightened by "combing." The thermostat may be on an adjacent wall or in the unit itself.

9.7 Central Air Conditioning

Central air-conditioning systems are defined as electrically operated refrigerant-type systems used for cooling and dehumidification. Heat pumps are similar to central air conditioners, but are reversible and can also be used as heating devices. Air-conditioning systems should be operated only when the outside air temperature is above 65° F; below that temperature, the system will not operate properly, may shut down due to safety controls, and could be damaged by operating in cool temperatures.

Air Conditioning System

EVAPORATOR COIL IN PLENUM

FREON IS LIQUID

EXPANSION DEVICE

FURNACE

BLOWER MOTOR

55°F

AIR FLOW

75 F

FREON IS GAS 100°F

OUTDOOR CONDENSER UNIT

FAN

CONDENSING COIL

85°F

FREON IS LIQUID

There are two types of central air-conditioning systems: integral and split. In the integral system, all mechanized components (compressor, condenser, evaporator and fans) are contained in a single unit. The unit may be located outside the building with its cold-air ductwork extending into the interior, or it may be located somewhere inside the building with its exhaust air ducted to the outside.

In the split system, the compressor and condenser are located outside the building and are connected by refrigerant lines to an evaporator inside the building's air-distribution ductwork. Split systems in buildings heated by forced warm air usually share the warm-air system's circulating fan and ductwork. In such cases, the evaporator is placed either directly above or below the furnace, depending on the furnace design.

Compressor and condenser. The compressor pumps refrigerant gas under high pressure through a condenser coil. Compressors have a service life of 12 to 15 years and are the most critical component in the air-conditioning system.

3 feet of clearance. If the compressor, condenser, and condenser fan are part of a split system and are located in a separate unit outside, check the air flow around the outside unit to make sure it is not obstructed.

Pay attention to the compressor. It should start smoothly and run continuously; noisy start-up and operation indicate a worn compressor. The condenser fan should start simultaneously with the compressor. After several minutes of operation, the air flowing over the condenser (the unit outside on a split system) should be warm. If it isn't, either the compressor may be faulty or there may not be enough refrigerant in the system.

Look inside and check for dirt and debris, particularly on the condenser coils and fins, and look at the electrical wiring and connections. The unit should be level and well-supported. Outdoor units often settle or slide. An electrical disconnect switch for use during maintenance and repairs should be located within sight of the exterior unit and not located behind the unit.

Refrigerant lines. Refrigerant lines form the link between the interior and exterior components of a split system. The larger of the two lines carries low-pressure (cold) refrigerant gas from the evaporator to the compressor. It is about the diameter of a broom handle and should be insulated along its entire length. The smaller line is not insulated and carries high-pressure (warm) liquid refrigerant to the evaporator.

Touch the lines. While the unit is operating, the smaller line should feel warm, and the larger should feel cool to the touch. You could check both lines for signs of damage and make sure the insulation is intact on the larger line. Sometimes, a sight glass is provided on the smaller line; if so, the flow of refrigerant should look smooth through the glass. Bubbles in the flow indicate a deficiency of refrigerant in the system. Frost on any exposed parts of the larger line also indicates a refrigerant deficiency.

Evaporator. The evaporator is enclosed in the air-distribution ductwork and can only be observed by removing a panel or part of the furnace plenum. High-pressure liquid refrigerant enters the evaporator and expands into a gas, absorbing heat from the surrounding air.

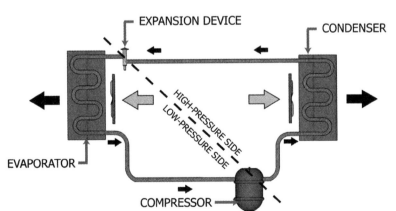

Refrigeration Cycle

EXPANSION DEVICE — CONDENSER — EVAPORATOR — HIGH-PRESSURE SIDE — LOW-PRESSURE SIDE — COMPRESSOR

Air is pushed past the evaporator coil by the circulation blower; in the process, water vapor from the air condenses on the evaporator coil and drips into a drain pan. From there,

it is directed to a condensate drain line, which may sometimes include a condensate pump. The drain line could empty into a house drain or be discharged to the building's exterior.

Monitor the ductwork around the evaporator for signs of air leakage, and check below the evaporator for signs of water leakage due to a blocked condensate drain line. Such leakage can present a serious problem if the evaporator is located above a warm-air furnace, where dripping condensate water can cause rust to develop on the heat exchanger, or above a ceiling, where it can damage the building components below. Follow the condensate line and make sure that it terminates in a proper location.

In a split system whose evaporator is located in an attic or closet, the condensate drain pan should have an auxiliary condensate drain line located above the regular drain line that should drain into a water-leak catch pan. The auxiliary drain pan that is separately drained should discharge to an area that is conspicuous. If you see this pipe leaking water, this indicates a problem.

Geothermal heating and cooling systems. Geothermal systems are relatively new and operate similarly to air-to-air heat-pump systems, but they differ in design and installation. What might be considered the condenser are pipes buried in the ground in dry wells or other in-ground systems suitable for transferring or displacing heat. The system is closed and its piping is made of PVC, so corrosion is not a potential problem. Geothermal systems are normally installed without a back-up or emergency heating system, and all their components (except the buried coils) are usually inside the house.

A geothermal heating and cooling system can be operated in a heating or cooling mode under any outside temperature. Although expensive to install, it is normally efficient and economical to operate.

9.8 Central Gas-Absorption Cooling System

Gas-absorption cooling systems may be found in older residential buildings. Such a system uses the evaporation of a liquid (such as ammonia) as the cooling agent and, like a gas refrigerator, is powered by a natural-gas or propane flame. It should start smoothly and run quietly.

9.9 Heat Pump

Heat pumps are like central air conditioners that can operate in reverse. Electric heat pumps are electrically operated, refrigerant-type air-conditioning systems that can be reversed to extract heat from the outside air and transfer it indoors.

Cold temperatures. Do not operate air-to-air heat pumps in outdoor temperatures below 65° F on the cooling cycle and above 66° F on the heating cycle. Electric-resistance auxiliary heaters are designed to activate when the outdoor temperature is around 30° F, and the air-to-air heat pump cannot produce enough heat to satisfy the thermostat.

Improper defrosting. During cold, damp weather, frost or ice may form on the metal fins of the coil in an outdoor unit. Heat pumps are designed to defrost this buildup by reversing modes either at preset intervals or upon activation by a pressure-sensing device.

9.10 Evaporative Cooling System

Evaporative cooling systems (also called swamp coolers) are simple and economical devices. They pass air through wetted pads or screens and cooling takes place by evaporation. Such systems can only be used in dry climates where evaporation readily takes place and where dehumidification is not required.

Evaporative coolers consist of evaporator pads or screens, a means to wet them, an air blower, and a water reservoir with a drain and float-operated water-supply valve. These components are contained in a single housing, usually located on the roof, and connected to an interior air-distribution system. In wetted-pad coolers, evaporator pads are wetted by a circulating pump that continually trickles water over them; in slinger coolers, evaporator pads are wetted by a spray; and in rotary coolers, evaporator screens are wetted by passing through a reservoir on a rotating drum.

The water in evaporative coolers often contains algae and bacteria that emit a characteristic swampy odor. These can be easily removed with bleach. Some systems counteract this pattern by treating the water or by continually adding a small amount of fresh water.

Monitor for signs of leakage and check the cleanliness and operation of the water reservoir, float-operated supply valve, and drain. Listen for unusual sounds or vibrations.

9.11 Humidifier

Humidifiers require consistent maintenance. Do not delay cleaning the humidifier because a dirty humidifier can cause air-quality problems.

A humidifier should only operate when the furnace fan is on, the system is in the heating mode, and the indoor humidity is lower than the humidistat setting.

Humidifiers are sometimes added to warm-air heating systems to reduce interior dryness during the heating season. They are installed with the air-distribution system and are controlled by a humidistat that is usually located in the return-air duct near the humidifier housing.

Types of humidifiers:

Stationary pad: Air is drawn from the furnace plenum or supply-air duct by a fan, blown over an evaporator pad, and returned to the air-distribution system.

Revolving drum: Water from a small reservoir is picked up by a revolving pad and exposed to an air stream from the furnace plenum or supply ductwork.

Atomizer: Water is broken into small particles by an atomizing device and released into the supply-air ductwork.

Drum-Type Humidifier

Steam: Water is heated to temperatures above boiling and then injected into the supply-air duct.

Monitor for mineral build-up on the drum or pad. Examine the humidifier's water supply and look for signs of leakage, especially at its connection with the house water supply. Check all electrical wiring and connections.

9.12 Unit (Window) Air Conditioners

Unit air conditioners are portable, integral air-conditioning systems without ductwork. Look at the seal around each unit and its attachment to the window or wall. It should be adequately supported. It should not be obstructed. Look for proper condensate drainage. After several minutes of operation, the air from the unit should feel quite cool. It should start smoothly and run quietly. Check for water dripping from the condensate discharge on the exterior of the unit.

9.13 Whole-House Fan

Whole-House Fan

The louvers of the whole-house fan should open completely when the fan is running. Clean the louvers when they are dirty. Be sure to cover the fan opening when the unit is not being used, especially during the winter in cold climates. The fan thermostat should be set at around 95° F. The fan should start and run smoothly.

According to the Standards of Practice:

The HVAC system is inspected using normal operating controls. The inspector is not required to inspect flues or chimneys, fire chambers, heat exchangers, humidifiers, electronic air filters, or geothermal systems. Underground or concealed fuel-storage systems are beyond the visual scope of a home inspection. The inspector is not required to check uniformity, BTU, temperature, flow, balance, distribution, or adequacy of the HVAC system. The inspector is not required to activate a system that has been shut down. An inspector is not required to operate the cooling system when the weather is cold, or operate the heating system when the weather is hot.

Chapter 10: Making Your Home Energy-Efficient

Sealing and insulating your home is one of the most cost-effective ways to make your home more comfortable and energy-efficient—and you can do it yourself.

You will notice your home's air leaks in the winter more than at any other time of year. Most people call these air leaks drafts. You may feel these drafts around windows and doors and think these leaks are your major source of wasted energy. In most homes, however, the most significant air leaks are hidden in the attic and basement. These are the leaks that significantly raise your energy bills and make your house uncomfortable.

In cold weather, warm air rises in your house, just like it does in a chimney. This air, which you have paid to heat, is just wasted as it rises up into your attic and sucks cold air in all around your home—around windows, doors, and through holes into the basement. Locating these leaks can be difficult because they are often hidden under the insulation.

An inspector who is certified in thermography and building science can help find these air leaks.

10.1 Getting Started

Sealing attic air leaks will enhance the performance of your home's insulation and make for a much more comfortable home.

If your attic is accessible and not too difficult to move around in, you can seal air leaks and add insulation yourself. This kind of project can be completed in one or two days and will provide rewards for years to come.

If you find any major problems in the attic space, such as roof leaks, mold, unsafe conditions, inadequate flooring, inadequate ventilation, knob-and-tube wiring, and/or recessed can lights, it is recommended that you hire a contractor to help you to correct these problems before proceeding.

Look around your house for any dropped-ceiling areas, dropped soffits over kitchen cabinets, slanted ceilings over stairways, and locations where walls (interior and exterior) meet the ceiling. These areas may have open spaces that could be huge sources of air leaks.

10.2 Working in the Attic

Be sure to use a work light to make sure that your work area is adequately lit.

Use personal protective equipment. To work in an attic, you need kneepads, coveralls, gloves and a hat to keep itchy and irritating insulation off your skin. Use an OSHA-approved particulate respirator or a high-quality dust mask.

Be safe. Do not work in the attic area if you feel that it is dangerous in any way. It's not worth risking life or property. Simply hire a qualified contractor to perform the work you need to get done. If you work in a hot attic, drink plenty of water.

Watch your step. Walk on joists or truss chords. Watch your head; there will be sharp nails and things sticking out above you and all around your head.

10.3 What You Will Need

- reflective foil insulation or other blocking material, such as drywall or pieces of rigid foam insulation, to cover soffits, open walls, and larger holes;

- unfaced fiberglass insulation;

- large garbage bags;

- silicone or acrylic latex caulk for sealing small holes (1/4-inch or smaller);

- expanding spray-foam insulation for filling larger gaps (1/4-inch to 3 inches);

- special high-temperature (heat-resistant) caulk to seal around flues and chimneys;

- a roll of aluminum flashing to keep insulation away from the flue pipe;

- tape measure;

- utility knife and sheet metal scissors; and

- staple gun (or hammer and nails) to hold covering materials in place.

10.4 Plug the Large Holes

The biggest savings will come from sealing the large holes. Locate the areas in the attic where leakage is likely to be greatest: where walls (interior and exterior) meet the attic floor; dropped soffits (dropped-ceiling areas); and behind or under attic knee walls. Look for dirty insulation. Dirty insulation (black/brown stains on the underside of the insulation) indicates that air is moving through it. Push back the insulation or pull it out of the soffits. You will place this insulation back over the soffit once the stud cavities have been plugged and the soffits covered.

Dropped soffit. After removing insulation from a dropped soffit, cut a length of reflective foil or other blocking material (rigid foamboard works well). Apply a bead of caulk or adhesive around the opening. Seal the foil to the frame with the caulk/adhesive and staple or nail it in place, if needed.

Under a wall. Cut a 24-inch long piece from a batt of fiberglass insulation and place it at the bottom of a 13-gallon plastic garbage bag. Fold the bag over and stuff it into the open joist spaces under the wall. A piece of rigid foamboard sealed with spray foam also works well for covering open joist cavities. Cover it with insulation when you're done.

 Finished rooms built into attics often have open cavities in the floor framing under the sidewalls or knee walls. Even though insulation may be piled against or stuffed into these spaces, they can still leak air. Again, look for signs of dirty insulation to indicate that air is moving through. You need to plug these cavities in order to stop air from traveling under the floor of the finished space.

Flue. The opening around the flue or chimney of a furnace or water heater can be a major source of warm air moving in the attic. Because the pipe gets hot, building codes usually require 1 inch of clearance from metal flues (or 2 inches from masonry chimneys) to any combustible material, including insulation. This gap can be sealed with lightweight aluminum flashing and special high-temperature (heat-resistant) caulk. Before you push the insulation back into place, build a barrier out of the metal aluminum to keep the insulation away from the pipe.

10.5 Seal the Small Holes

Look for areas where the insulation is darkened. This is the result of dusty air coming from the house's interior and moving into and being filtered by the insulation. In cold weather, you may also see frosty areas in the insulation caused by warm, moist air condensing and then freezing as it hits the cold attic air. In warmer weather, you'll find water staining in these same areas. Use expanding foam or caulk to seal the openings around plumbing vent pipes and electrical wires. When the foam or caulk is dry, cover the area again with insulation. After sealing the areas, just push the insulation back into place. If you have blown insulation, a small hand tool can be helpful to level it back into place.

10.6 Attic Access

Seal up the attic access panel with weatherstripping. Cut a piece of fiberglass or rigid foamboard insulation the same size as the attic hatch and glue it to the back of the attic access panel.

If you have pull-down attic stairs or an attic door, these should be sealed in a similar manner using weatherstripping and insulating the back of the door. Treat the attic door like an exterior door to the outside.

10.7 Ducts

Sealing and insulating your ducts can increase the efficiency of your HVAC system. Leaky ducts waste an incredible amount of energy. Check the duct connections for leaks and seal the joints with mastic or foil tape (household duct tape should not be used). Pay special attention to all the duct penetrations going through the attic floor. Seal these with foam.

HVAC ducts should also be insulated—if your ducts are uninsulated or poorly insulated, seal them first, then add insulation. Use duct insulation material rated at least R-6. Duct sealant, also known as duct mastic, is a paste, which is more durable than foil duct tape. It is available at home improvement centers.

10.8 Can Lights

Recessed can lights (also called high-hats or recessed lights) can make your home less energy-efficient. These recessed lights can create open holes that allow unwanted air flow from conditioned spaces to unconditioned spaces. In cold climates, the heat from the air flow can melt snow on the roof and cause the development of ice dams. Recessed can lights in bathrooms also cause problems when warm, moist air leaks into the attic and causes moisture damage.

WARNING: You can create a fire hazard if the can light is not insulated or sealed properly. It may be best to consult a professional before sealing can lights or coming in contact with any electrical components.

10.9 Stack Effect

Like a chimney. Outside air drawn in through open holes and gaps in the basement is drawn in by a stack effect created by air leaks in the attic. As hot air generated by the furnace rises up through the house and into the attic through open holes, cold outside air gets drawn in through open holes in the basement to replace the displaced air. This makes a home feel drafty and contributes to higher energy bills. After sealing attic air leaks, complete the job by sealing basement leaks to stop the stack effect.

Basement air leaks. A good area to look for open holes and gaps is along the top of the basement wall where the floor system meets the top of the foundation wall. Since the top of the wall is above ground, outside air can be drawn in through cracks and gaps where the house framing sits on top of the foundation.

Sealant or caulk is best for sealing gaps or cracks that are 1/4-inch or less. Use spray foam to fill gaps from 1/4-inch to about 3 inches. It is recommend that you seal penetrations that go through the basement ceiling to the floor above. These are holes for wires, water supply pipes, water drainpipes, the plumbing vent stack, and the furnace flue.

Attic and basement air sealing will go a long way to improve your comfort because your house will no longer act like an open chimney.

10.10 Attic Insulation Thickness

Look. One quick way to determine if you need more insulation on the floor of your attic is to simply look across the floor of your attic. If the insulation is level with or below your floor joists, more insulation is needed. If the insulation is well above the joists, you may have enough. There should be no low spots.

R-Value. Insulation levels are specified by R-value. R-value is a measure of insulation's ability to resist heat flow. The higher the R-value, the better the thermal performance of the insulation. The recommended level for most attic floors is R-38 or about 10 to 14 inches, depending on the type of insulation and your climate.

When adding insulation, you do not have to use the same type of insulation that currently exists in your attic. You can add loose-fill on top of fiberglass batts or blankets, and vice versa. If you use fiberglass over loose-fill, make sure the fiberglass batt has no paper or foil vapor barrier. The insulation needs to be unfaced.

Laying out or spreading fiberglass rolls is easy. If you have any type of insulation between the rafters, install the second layer over and perpendicular to the first. This will help cover the tops of the joists and reduce heat loss and gain through the frame.

NEVER! Never lay insulation over recessed light fixtures or soffit vents. Keep all insulation at least 3 inches away from can lights, unless they are IC-rated (insulated ceiling). If you are using loose-fill insulation, use sheet metal to create barriers around the openings. If using fiberglass, wire mesh can be used to create a barrier.

Rafter vent trays. To completely cover your attic floor with insulation out to the eaves, you need to install rafter vents or trays, also called insulation baffles. Rafter vents ensure that the soffit vents are clear and there is a clear opening for outside air to move into the attic at the soffits and out through the gable or ridge vents for proper ventilation.

10.11 A Last Word About Your Home's Energy

Did you know that the typical U.S. family spends about $2,200 a year on their home's utility bills?

Unfortunately, a large portion of that energy is wasted. And each year, electricity generated by fossil fuels for a single home puts more carbon dioxide into the air than two average cars. The good news is that there is a lot you can do to save energy and money at home.

The key to achieving these savings in your home is a whole-house energy-efficiency plan. To take a whole-house approach, view your home as an energy system with interdependent parts. For example, your heating system is not just a furnace—it's a heat-delivery system that starts at the furnace and delivers heat throughout your home using a network of ducts. Even a top-of-the-line, energy-efficient furnace will waste a lot of fuel if the ducts, walls, attic, windows and doors are not properly sealed and insulated. Taking a whole-house approach to saving energy ensures that the dollars you invest to save energy are spent wisely.

Energy-efficient improvements not only make your home more comfortable, they can yield long-term financial rewards. Reduced utility bills more than make up for the higher price of energy-efficient appliances and improvements over their lifetimes. In addition, your home could bring in a higher price when you sell.

The first step to taking a whole-house energy-efficiency approach is to find out which parts of your house use the most energy. A home energy inspection will pinpoint those areas and provide the most effective measures for cutting your energy costs. You can conduct a simple home energy inspection yourself, contact your local utility, or call an InterNACHI-Certified Energy Inspector for a more comprehensive assessment.

Once you assign priorities to your energy needs, you can form a whole-house efficiency plan. Your plan will provide you with a strategy for making smart purchases and home improvements that maximize energy efficiency and save the most money.

Another option is to get the advice of a professional. A professional contractor can analyze how well your home's energy systems work together and compare the analysis to your utility bills. He or she will use a variety of equipment, such as blower doors, infrared cameras, and surface thermometers to find leaks and drafts. After gathering information about your home, the contractor or auditor will give you a list of recommendations for cost-effective energy improvements and enhanced comfort and safety. A reputable contractor can also calculate the return on your investment in high-efficiency equipment compared with standard equipment.

Be sure to hire an InterNACHI-Certified Home Energy Inspector, who abides by a Code of Ethics that prevents him or her from working on the property they inspect and, without exception, does not allow conflicts of interest to exist.

To find a Home Energy Inspector, visit **www.nachi.org/go/find**

Appendix I: Seasonal Maintenance Checklist

These are checklists that you can use and incorporate into your regular maintenance program for your house.

 In the Spring:

- Check for damage to your roof.
- Check all the fascia and trim for deterioration.
- Have an HVAC professional inspect and maintain your system as recommended by the manufacturer.
- Check your water heater for leaks or rust.
- Check your fire extinguishers.
- Clean the kitchen exhaust hood and air filter.
- Repair all cracked, broken and uneven driveways and walks to help provide a level walking surface.
- Check the shutoff valves at all plumbing fixtures to make sure they function.
- Clean the clothes dryer exhaust duct and damper, and the space under the dryer.

 In the Summer:

- Check kids' playground equipment.
- Check your wood deck or concrete patio for deterioration.
- Check the nightlights at the top and bottom of all stairways.
- Check the exterior siding.
- Check all window and door locks.
- Check your home for water leaks.
- Check the water hoses on the clothes washer, refrigerator, icemaker and dishwasher for cracks and bubbles.

 **In the Fall:**

- Have a heating professional check your heating system.
- Protect your home from frozen pipes.
- Run all gas-powered lawn equipment until the fuel is gone.
- Test your emergency generator.
- Have a certified chimney sweep inspect and clean the flues and check your fireplace damper.
- Remove birds' nests from chimney flues and outdoor electrical fixtures.
- Make sure the caulking around doors and windows is adequate to reduce heating/cooling loss.
- Make sure that the caulking around the bathroom fixtures is adequate to prevent water from seeping into the sub-flooring.
- Clean the gutters and downspouts.

 In the Winter:

- Confirm that firewood is stored at least 20 feet away from your home.
- Remove screens from windows and install storm windows.
- Familiarize responsible family members with the gas main valve and other appliance valves.
- Make sure all electrical holiday decorations have tight connections.
- Test all AFCI and GFCI devices.
- Only when it is safe to do so, occasionally check for ice-dam formation in the gutters.

 Annually:

- Review your emergency escape plan with your family.
- Make sure your house number is visible from the street for first-responders to see.
- Replace all extension cords that have become brittle, worn or damaged.
- Inspect and clean dust from the covers of your smoke detectors and carbon-monoxide alarms.
- Have your InterNACHI-Certified Professional Inspector® perform a yearly home maintenance inspection.

Appendix II: Service Life Expectancies

Appliance	Life Expectancy in Years
Air-conditioner compressor	12-15
Asphalt, wood shingles/shakes	15-40
Asphalt composition shingles	15-40
Asphalt driveways	8-12
Baseboard heating systems	15-25
Boilers, hot-water or steam	25-35
Brick and concrete patios	15-25
Brick and stone walls	100+
Built-up roofing, asphalt	10-26
Central air-conditioning unit	12-15
Concrete block foundations	100+
Concrete walks	10-20
Dishwashers	8-10
Dryers	8-14
Electric ranges	14-18
Electric water heaters	5-12
Exhaust fans	5-10
Faucets	10-15
Fences	10-15
Floor tile	30-40+
Forced-air furnaces, heat pumps	12-18
Freezers, standard	10-20
Furnaces, gas- and oil-fired	15-20
Garage door openers	8-12
Garage doors	20-25
Garbage disposals	8-10
Gas ovens	10-18
Gas ranges	12-20
Gas water heaters	6-12

Appliance	Life Expectancy in Years
Gravel walks	4-6
Gutters and downspouts	25-30
Heat exchangers	10-15
Humidifiers	5-7
Microwave ovens	9-13
Poured concrete foundations	100+
Pumps, sump and well	5-12
Refrigerators	10-18
Rooftop air conditioners	14-18
Sheet metal	20-50
Siding, aluminum	20-40
Siding, steel	30-50
Siding, vinyl	30-45
Siding, wood	12-100
Sinks, China	15-20
Sinks, enamel-coated cast-iron	20-30
Sinks, enamel-coated steel	5-10
Slate roof tiles	40-100
Smoke detectors	5-10
Sprinkler systems	10-14
Stucco	20-40+
Swimming pools	10-20
Termite-proofing	5-7
Trash compactors	6-10
Tile	30-40+
Washers, clothes	12-16
Waste piping, cast-iron	50-100
Window A/C units	5-8
Wooden decks	12-20

Appendix III: Water Management and Damage Prevention

This section provides homeowners with basic information on how to make smart decisions and take the appropriate actions to keep their homes dry and comfortable.

Designing, building and maintaining homes that manage moisture effectively are a process of making good decisions.

While builders and designers provide most of the up-front decisions, such as designing the roof system or specifying the foundation drainage details, over the long term, the homeowner must understand basic moisture issues and make good decisions at the right times.

There is already plenty of useful guidance for homeowners on what to do (and not do) regarding moisture. This chapter does not "reinvent the wheel" but will instead rely on available guidance for homeowners.

Most (if not all) moisture-related problems could become serious and expensive if not taken care of quickly and completely.

Houses and water. Water, in its many forms, is an ever-present fact of life for a homeowner. Households can use hundreds of gallons of tap water on a daily basis. Lots of rainwater must be successfully shed by the roof and siding during rainstorms. Groundwater moves through the soil beneath the foundation. Indoor humidity levels are controlled for comfort. Moisture in the forms of condensation and water vapor is absorbed and released by the house itself.

When a well-built home is properly maintained, water is a benefit and a pleasure. On the other hand, uncontrolled water in our homes can cause damage. It can lead to mold growth, rotten wood and structural damage.

It repels excess water. The exterior surfaces of a house, from roof to foundation, make up its envelope or "skin." The skin is designed to shed or repel excess water. If it doesn't, expect trouble. When roof flashings, windows, foundation walls, and other building components are not properly maintained, rainwater will find its way into vulnerable parts of the house.

It absorbs and releases excess moisture. All houses must absorb and release moisture constantly in order to maintain a healthy balance. If the house has "breathing problems," many types of moisture problems can develop. Trapped moisture (dampness that cannot be released, for one reason or another) is one of the primary causes of fungus and mold growth in a house. Fungi can literally eat wood, causing decay, rot and, ultimately, structural damage. Trapped moisture in the walls can destroy the value of the insulation and raise heating and cooling costs. Wood that stays damp attracts carpenter ants and other insects that can accelerate structural problems.

It transports piped water. Directly beneath the skin of the house is a complex maze of pipes carrying fresh water through the house and drain lines to dispose of water after its use. There are dozens of pipe joints and specialized fittings throughout the house, any one of which can develop a leak and cause moisture damage.

It needs a firm, dry foundation. The best foundation is a dry foundation. A water-damaged foundation is extremely expensive to repair and can lead to damage in the rest of the house. Groundwater, flood water, or even rainwater from a misdirected downspout can undermine the foundation and cause settling cracks, wet floors and walls and lead to undesirable conditions.

Frequent causes of moisture damage.
Unwanted water can intrude through cracks in the protective skin of the house. It can also accumulate from interior moisture sources.

The most common sources of moisture problems at the exterior a house include:

Roof and flashing. Roofing materials can wear out, break, rust, blow off, or otherwise fail and expose the roof deck and structural components beneath to moisture intrusion and damage.

Most leaks occur around penetrations through the roof, such as at a chimney, plumbing vent, exhaust fan or skylight. Flashings and sealant joints around these penetrations can crack, fail and leak. Intersections of roof surfaces with walls are also a common leakage point.

Old or defective shingles can curl and crack, allowing moisture intrusion. If old shingles aren't removed before new roof shingles are installed, this can reduce the life of the new roof. Chimney caps can crack, allowing water into interior areas of the chimney.

Shingle edges can fail, forcing rainwater to accumulate between the roof and gutter.

Flat and low-pitched roofs have unique maintenance needs and are susceptible to water problems because they may not drain as quickly as roofs with a steeper pitch.

Flat roof drains or scuppers can clog and hold water on the roof, increasing the risk not only of a leak, but also of a possible collapse of the entire roof under the weight of the water.

Gutters and downspouts. Clogged gutters can force rainwater to travel up onto the roof under shingles, or to overflow and travel down the inside of the wall, or to overflow and collect at the home's foundation.

First-floor gutters can overflow if second-floor gutters have been mistakenly directed to drain into them.

Undersized or an insufficient number of downspouts can cause gutters to overflow. Downspouts that don't empty far enough away from foundation walls can lead to foundation wall damage and a wet basement.

Ice dams. Inadequate attic insulation allows heat to escape from the house into the attic, which can turn rooftop snow into an ice dam along the eaves. Ice dams frequently force moisture to back up under the roof shingles where it can drip into the attic or walls.

Clogged or frozen gutters can act like ice dams, pushing moisture up under the shingles and into the house.

Soffits and fascias. Damaged soffits (horizontal surfaces under the eaves) can allow snow or rain to be blown into the attic, damaging the insulation, ceilings and walls. Fascia boards (vertical roof-trim sections) can be damaged, allowing the moisture from rain and snow into the attic and atop interior walls.

Weep holes. Weep holes, which are designed to allow moisture to escape from behind walls, can become blocked.

Weep holes can freeze, forcing moisture to back up inside the wall cavity.

Weep holes can become clogged with landscape mulch, soil and other material.

Landscaping and grading. Recent landscape modifications may result in water drainage back toward the foundation, rather than away from it.

A newly-built home lot may have been graded improperly, or the original foundation backfill may have settled over time, and this can cause drainage problems.

Automatic sprinklers may be spraying water onto or too close to the foundation walls.

Window and door flashing and seals. Cracked, torn or damaged seals, weatherstripping, and flashing around windows and doors can allow wind-blown moisture to penetrate your house.

Improperly installed windows and doors can allow moisture into the wall.

Failed or worn weatherstripping can allow wind-driven rain to penetrate a closed window or door.

Groundwater and rainwater. Groundwater and misdirected rainwater can collect during wet seasons along the foundation wall or beneath the floor or slab. Unless it is directed away from the structure by a sump pump or corrected drainage, this moisture can lead to mold growth, wall failure, and other destructive moisture problems.

Condensation. Condensation on windows can, at a minimum, damage windowsills and finishes. At worst, it can damage walls and floors, as well. Condensation on un-insulated pipes can collect nearby or travel along a pipe to accumulate far from the original source.

Condensation can form inside improperly built walls and lead to serious water damage and biological growth that are hidden from sight.

HVAC. Lapses in regular maintenance can lead to moisture and comfort problems, ranging from clogged drain pans to iced-up cooling coils and mold within the system.

Failure to clean and service air conditioners regularly can lead to diminishing performance, higher operating costs, and potential moisture problems.

Humidifiers can add too much moisture to a house, leading to dampness and mold.

Sump pump. Neglecting to test a sump pump routinely, especially if it is rarely used, can lead to severe water damage when a heavy storm, snow melt, or flooding sends water against the home.

Overload of the sump pump due to poor drainage elsewhere on the property can lead to pump failure. Frequent sump operation can be a sign of excessive water buildup under the basement floor due to poorly sloped landscaping, poor rain runoff, gutter back-flows, and other problems.

Lack of a back-up sump pump, which can be quickly installed in the event the first pump fails, can lead to serious water damage and property loss. This is especially important if the sump pump is relied upon to maintain a dry basement, or if the house is located in an area of seasonally high groundwater. Sump failure can cause extensive water damage and the loss of valuable personal belongings.

Appendix IV: Consumer Resources

InterNACHI®

The world's largest association of certified professional home and commercial property inspectors: www.nachi.org

Certified Professional Inspectors®

Find all of the best inspectors in one place: www.nachi.org/find

IAC2

International Association of Certified Indoor Air Consultants: IAC2.org

MoveInCertified.com

MoveInCertified homes have been pre-inspected by InterNACHI® Certified Professional Inspectors® and the sellers confirm that there are no major systems in need of immediate repair or replacement, and no known safety hazards. Visit MoveInCertified.com

OverSeeIt.com

Replacing a roof? Having a new home built? Remodeling a bathroom? Adding a deck? We'll make sure your contractor does it right! Visit OverSeeIt.com

PRO-LAB

Contact the world's largest environmental testing laboratory: www.nachi.org/go/prolab

Location of Major Home Components:

HVAC System   (year: _____)

   • Air Filter _____

   • Shut-Off Switch _____

   • Shut-Off Valve _____

Plumbing

   • Hot Water Source _____   (size: _____)

      – Electric Shut-Off Switch _____

      – Fuel Shut-Off Valve _____

      – Water Shut-Off Valve _____

   • Main Water Shut-Off Valve _____

   • DWV Clean-Out Pipe _____

   • Septic Tank _____   (year: _____)

   • Private Water Well _____

Electrical

   • Main Panelboard _____

   • Main Disconnect _____

   • GFCI/AFCI _____

Fire Extinguisher _____   (year: _____)

Maintenance Notes:

To be addressed as soon as possible:

_____

_____

_____

_____

_____

To be addressed before the weather changes:

_____

_____

_____

_____

_____

To consider and budget for long-term:

_____

_____

_____

_____

_____

Final Walk-Through Checklist

This checklist will help you and your InterNACHI home inspector do a final assessment of the condition of the home just before you finalize the paperwork for the sale. Also noted may be items reported at your initial inspection as in need of repair or replacement by the seller. If there is an agreement to leave or remove certain appliances, fixtures, or household articles, these can be confirmed, too.

Room, Area and/or Item	Leave Behind	Remove Item	N/A	Tested as Operational	Defect Not Previously Noted
Kitchen					
Refrigerator					
Stove/Range					
Microwave					
Dishwasher					
Trash Compactor					
Flooring					
Walls					
Other:					
Laundry					
Washer					
Dryer					
Water Softener					
Utility Sink					
Other:					
Bathroom (if multiple, specify location)					
Towel Rack/Cabinets					
Toilet					
Sink					
Shower/Tub					
Floor/Walls					
Other:					
Bedroom (if multiple, specify location)					
Affixed Mirrors					

Room, Area and/or Item	Leave Behind	Remove Item	N/A	Tested as Operational	Defect Not Previously Noted
Carpets/Rugs					
Walls					
Other:					
Living Room/Dining Room/Den/Office (specify location)					
Carpets/Rugs					
Walls					
Other:					
HVAC					
Thermostat					
Filter					
Other:					
Electrical					
Receptacles					
Lights					
Other:					
Plumbing					
Attic					
Basement/Crawlspace					
Garage					
Exterior					
Sprinkler System					

Don't forget to schedule your Annual Home Maintenance Inspection!

Even the most vigilant homeowner can, from time to time, miss small problems or forget about performing some routine home repairs and seasonal maintenance. That's why an Annual Home Maintenance Inspection will help you keep your home in good condition and prevent it from suffering serious, long-term and expensive damage from minor issues that should be addressed now.

The most important thing to understand as a new homeowner is that your house requires care and regular maintenance. As time goes on, parts of your house will wear out, break down, deteriorate, leak, or simply stop working. But none of these issues means that you will have a costly disaster on your hands if you're on top of home maintenance, and that includes hiring an expert once a year.

Just as you regularly maintain your vehicle, consider getting an Annual Home Maintenance Inspection as part of the cost of upkeep for your most valuable investment—your home.

Your InterNACHI-Certified Professional Inspector® can show you what you should look for so that you can be an informed homeowner. Protect your family's health and safety, and enjoy your home for years to come by having an Annual Home Maintenance Inspection performed every year.

Use the following space to record any questions or concerns that you would like addressed during your Annual Home Maintenance Inspection:

My Inspector: